Helm for Kubernetes Deployment

Definitive Reference for Developers and Engineers

Richard Johnson

Contents

4

5

6

Introduction

The landscape of container orchestration has been fundamentally transformed by Kubernetes, which has emerged as the preeminent platform for managing distributed, containerized applications. Its architecture, designed for scalability, resilience, and automation, provides the foundation upon which modern cloud-native applications are deployed and managed. Despite the robust capabilities Kubernetes offers, the complexities involved in deploying and maintaining applications at scale have necessitated sophisticated tooling to streamline these processes.

Helm, as the standard package manager for Kubernetes, addresses many challenges faced by operators and developers in configuring, packaging, and deploying applications. It introduces a level of abstraction and automation that simplifies interactions with Kubernetes resources through the use of charts—self-contained packages that describe a set of Kubernetes objects. Helm's ecosystem provides essential features such as templating, versioning, dependency management, and lifecycle control. These capabilities significantly reduce operational overhead, promote consistency, and facilitate collaboration across teams.

This book presents a comprehensive exploration of Helm and its integration within Kubernetes deployment workflows. It begins by elucidating foundational concepts, including Kubernetes architecture and the evolution of application management within this ecosystem, establishing the rationale for Helm's development and its pivotal role in the orchestration environment. Understanding these fundamentals ensures a strong grounding from which to appreciate the subsequent, more advanced concepts.

A detailed examination of Helm charts follows, dissecting their structure, best practices in authoring, and techniques to manage their lifecycle effectively. The emphasis on templating and configuration management equips readers with methodologies to build flexible, reusable, and maintainable charts. Advanced templating strategies and value management techniques are explored, providing the necessary tools to handle complex scenarios with precision and efficiency.

The management of secrets and sensitive data within Helm deployments is addressed critically, recognizing the importance of secure handling practices in modern infrastructures. Practical guidance on integrating native Kubernetes secrets, external secret managers, and GitOps secure workflows enhances the reader's ability to maintain compliance and security at scale.

Managing the release lifecycle encompasses installation, upgrades, rollbacks, and failure recovery mechanisms. This section delivers best practices to ensure reliability, availability, and operational excellence during deployments. In addition, it covers strategies for automated remediation and health monitoring, crucial for maintaining resilient applications.

Distribution and repository management of Helm charts are key areas for enabling collaboration and scalability within organizations. Discussions cover formats, authentication, signing, provenance, and integration into continuous integration and continuous delivery (CI/CD) pipelines. In this context, the book extends into the incorporation of Helm within GitOps methodologies, highlighting declarative infrastructure and automated promotion, which align with modern operational paradigms.

Security and compliance receive focused attention, covering access control, vulnerability management, auditing, and supply chain security. The principles and practices outlined assist practitioners in safeguarding their Kubernetes environments and ensuring that deployments adhere to organizational and regulatory standards.

Scaling Helm for multi-tenancy and performance is another essential aspect addressed. Techniques for chart design, resource isolation, performance optimization, and troubleshooting large-scale deployments prepare the reader to operate Helm in complex, enterprise-grade environments. The ecosystem of Helm plugins and extensions further extends its functionality to meet diverse operational requirements.

Finally, the book provides insight into emerging trends and future directions for Helm. It explores evolving standards, innovative deployment patterns, integration with advanced networking and service mesh technologies, cross-platform management strategies, and ongoing research in declarative security and drift remediation. The discussion concludes with reflections on Helm's positioning within the broader cloud-native community and its anticipated trajectory.

This comprehensive treatment is intended for practitioners, developers, and architects seeking an authoritative guide to mastering Helm for Kubernetes deployments. It balances conceptual clarity with pragmatic details, enabling readers to harness Helm's full potential to achieve efficient, secure, and scalable application delivery.

Chapter 1

Foundations of Kubernetes and Helm

Before we can harness the full power of Helm for deploying applications in Kubernetes, we must understand the architectural underpinnings and motivations that shaped both projects. This chapter reveals the interplay between Kubernetes' internal mechanics and the evolving needs of cloud-native application management, setting the stage for why Helm emerged as a cornerstone tool in orchestrating modern deployments. Whether you come from operations, development, or architecture, you'll discover not just how Kubernetes works, but why Helm has risen to be indispensable for scalable success.

1.1. Kubernetes Architecture Overview

Kubernetes is a sophisticated orchestration platform designed to automate deployment, scaling, and management of containerized applications. Its architecture is fundamentally composed of two main entity classes: the control plane (master components) and the worker nodes, each housing essential processes that collectively realize a dynamic and resilient system. The following exposition delves into the core components of these entities, underscoring their interactions and roles toward preserving the desired cluster state and workload lifecycle.

At the heart of the control plane, the **API Server** serves as the central management hub, exposing the Kubernetes API through a RESTful interface. All communication, whether from external clients, internal components, or users, predominately interacts via the API Server. It performs validation, authentication, and authorization, and persists cluster state in *etcd*, a strongly consistent distributed key-value store. The API Server thus functions as both the central data repository and the control nexus for cluster coordination.

The **Controller Manager** is a critical control plane process embodying a suite of controllers, each responsible for reconciling different aspects of cluster state. These controllers continuously monitor resource objects by querying the API Server; upon detecting deviations from the desired state, such as unscheduled pods or orphaned resources, they execute necessary corrective actions. For example, the Node Controller monitors node health, while the ReplicaSet Controller ensures the defined number of pod replicas are maintained. Collectively, these controllers implement the fundamental control loops that enable Kubernetes' self-healing and declarative management capabilities.

Complementing the Controller Manager is the **Scheduler**, tasked with assigning newly created pods to appropriate nodes within the cluster. The Scheduler evaluates node suitability based on constraints including resource availability (CPU, memory), affinity, taints, and other custom policies. Importantly, it interfaces with the API Server to retrieve unscheduled pods and node information, then updates the pod specification to reflect the selected node. This scheduling decision is instrumental in achieving optimal workload distribution and resource utilization in the cluster.

Transitioning to the node level, each worker node runs a set of key agents crucial for executing the scheduled workloads and maintaining communication with the control plane.

- The **kubelet** is the primary node agent responsible for managing pods assigned to that node. It registers the node with the cluster, periodically reports node and pod status back to the API Server, and ensures that containers defined in the PodSpecs are running and healthy. The kubelet interacts with the underlying container runtime (e.g., containerd, Docker) to launch and monitor container processes, thus functioning as the node's operational executor.

- Equally vital on each node is **kube-proxy**, a network proxy that maintains network rules facilitating communication to and from pods. It implements service abstraction by managing virtual IP addresses and load balancing traffic across backend pods associated with a Kubernetes Service. Operating at the network layer, kube-proxy leverages various mechanisms such as iptables or IP Virtual Server (IPVS) to route and forward packets efficiently, ensuring service discovery and connectivity within the cluster network fabric.

The cooperative operation of these components realizes Kubernetes' declarative model. Users define the desired cluster state declaratively via manifests or API objects. The API Server captures these definitions, persisting them in etcd. Controllers continually observe this state, comparing it with the current cluster state reported by kubelets and other node agents. Upon divergence, reconciliation loops restore alignment by creating or killing pods, updating configuration, or reallocating resources. This separation of concerns-with a centralized control plane and distributed node agents-enhances scalability, fault tolerance, and responsiveness.

Furthermore, the architecture supports extensibility through custom controllers and schedulers, enabling tailored automation beyond default behaviors. The extensible API also promotes integration with various systems and cloud providers, facilitating hybrid and multi-cloud deployments. Together, these architectural decisions underpin Kubernetes' robust ecosystem capable of managing complex application landscapes.

Kubernetes architecture is a concerted orchestration of master components and node agents, each specialized but interdependent. The API Server centralizes cluster state and communication; the Controller Manager and Scheduler enforce desired workload and node scheduling policies; while kubelet and kube-proxy on nodes execute workloads and foster seamless networking. This synergy ensures that Kubernetes continuously adapts to change and maintains the desired operational posture of containerized applications.

1.2. The Evolution of Kubernetes Application Management

Kubernetes initially provided a powerful yet low-level abstraction for container orchestration, relying heavily on declarative YAML manifests to define application configurations. These YAML files, although human-readable and expressive, encapsulated Kubernetes objects at a granularity that aligned closely with the underlying API resources such as Pods, Services, Deployments, and ConfigMaps. This approach, while flexible, required operators and developers to manually author and manage often large and intricate configuration sets. The growing adoption of Kubernetes revealed several challenges intrinsic to this primitive deployment method.

Early Kubernetes deployments exposed the necessity for repeatability and consistency. Manual editing of YAML files increased the probability of human error, as critical configuration elements such

8

as resource limits, probe settings, and volume mount points had to be replicated accurately across multiple manifests. There was also the issue of environment-specific customization, which initially demanded maintaining separate copies of nearly identical YAML files with minor variations for staging, production, and development clusters. This manual duplication escalated operational overhead and impeded standardization efforts.

As organizations scaled their Kubernetes use, the complexity of applications and the operational landscape intensified. Modern cloud-native applications often consist of multiple microservices with interdependent lifecycles, requiring coordinated updates, versioning, and rollback capabilities. This complexity revealed the limitations of raw YAML-based management. Without tooling abstraction, managing inter-related workloads and dependencies became error-prone and non-reproducible. The need for higher-order abstractions and templating systems became apparent in order to enforce standards, reduce duplication, and automate repetitive tasks.

One of the earliest advancements involved the introduction of templating engines like Helm. Helm emerged as a de facto package manager for Kubernetes, enabling users to define charts-parameterized, reusable templates encapsulating entire applications or service stacks. By separating static manifests from environment-specific values, Helm alleviated the challenge of duplication. It empowered users to deploy consistent configurations across clusters via values substitutions and to perform controlled upgrades and rollbacks with versioned chart releases. However, Helm's template language, based on Go templates, imposed limitations in expressiveness and logic control, occasionally producing complex and less maintainable charts as applications grew in sophistication.

Concurrently, domain-specific languages (DSLs) and frameworks began to flourish, aiming to model Kubernetes applications pro-

9

grammatically. Tools such as Kustomize offered a declarative way to patch and compose YAML files, simplifying customization through overlays rather than templates. Kustomize's imperative layering model allowed fine-grained modifications without duplicating base manifests, improving maintainability while remaining aligned with Kubernetes native objects. This marked an evolution from purely template-driven management to a more composable and declarative mindset.

Further advancement came with the rise of Infrastructure as Code (IaC) approaches integrated with higher-level programming languages and APIs. Projects like Pulumi and Crossplane introduced Kubernetes resource provisioning in languages such as TypeScript, Python, and Go, blending application deployment with infrastructure definition and management. This integration enabled developers to leverage familiar programming constructs-conditionals, loops, abstractions-to express complex application and infrastructure topologies as code, fostering improved modularity, reusable components, and testability.

The expanding Kubernetes ecosystem also necessitated robust lifecycle management mechanisms beyond initial deployment. Operators emerged as custom controllers extending the Kubernetes API, automating operational knowledge for applications, managing upgrades, backups, scaling policies, and failure recovery in a native, declarative manner. Operators embody the principle of embedding domain-specific logic into the control plane, enabling sophisticated, stateful workloads to benefit from Kubernetes automation. This paradigm shift addressed the operational complexity imposed by distributed systems, which basic manifest files could not encode effectively.

Beyond toolchains and APIs, organizational and procedural adaptations became equally critical. Continuous Integration and Continuous Deployment (CI/CD) pipelines evolved to integrate Kubernetes-native deployment steps, incorporating Helm,

Kustomize, or operator-based workflows. GitOps practices, in particular, enforced a declarative source of truth model, where application state is represented and versioned in Git repositories, enabling automated reconciliation by Kubernetes controllers. This model reinforces reproducibility, auditability, and rollback, further governing the application lifecycle from a centralized control point.

The evolution from manual YAML files to sophisticated application management frameworks reflects a fundamental response to the increasing complexity and scale of Kubernetes environments. Early simplicity gave way to structured abstractions embodied in templating engines, configuration layering tools, programmatic APIs, and custom controllers that automate operational knowledge. Each stage addresses unique pain points-be it reducing human error, managing configuration drift, enforcing domain-specific behaviors, or integrating with infrastructure provisioning and CI/CD pipelines.

As applications continue to grow in scale and heterogeneity, these advancements collectively enable more scalable, repeatable, and reliable Kubernetes operations. They underscore a critical insight: while Kubernetes provides a versatile foundation, effective application management requires tooling and methodologies that abstract complexity, codify best practices, and automate routine tasks, thus empowering organizations to harness Kubernetes at scale with confidence and agility.

1.3. Introduction to Helm: Motivation and Roles

Kubernetes has emerged as the de facto standard for container orchestration, providing a robust platform to deploy, scale, and manage containerized applications. However, as Kubernetes deployments scale in complexity, the need for a higher-level abstraction to manage application lifecycle and configuration becomes critical. Helm was conceived to address this necessity, fulfilling a pivotal role in automating and codifying Kubernetes deployments.

The motivations behind Helm stem from several intrinsic challenges present in traditional Kubernetes workflows. Initially, Kubernetes manifests—written as YAML configuration files—are verbose and declarative, requiring meticulous attention to detail. Managing multiple interdependent resources such as Deployments, Services, ConfigMaps, and Ingress objects quickly becomes unwieldy. For example, changing application parameters or upgrading versions necessitates manual edits across several files, increasing the risk of errors and inconsistencies. As environments move from development to staging and production, the burden of managing separate customized configurations for each environment further complicates the deployment process.

Existing workflows, prior to Helm, often relied on scripting or custom tooling to solve these problems but lacked standardization and reusability. The absence of a consistent packaging system meant that application components and their relationships were scattered, resulting in fragile and brittle deployment pipelines. Moreover, these approaches lacked a clear, repeatable method for versioning application configurations and tracking changes over time. This deficiency severely hindered the automation of complex deployments, a critical requirement for continuous delivery and continuous integration (CI/CD) processes.

Helm addresses these constraints by introducing the concept of a package manager tailored explicitly for Kubernetes. Its architecture encapsulates Kubernetes resources into a single unit called a *Chart*, which codifies all necessary objects and configuration templates into a coherent package. Helm Charts enable users to parameterize deployments using templating, thus allowing the reuse of a single base configuration that can be customized for multiple environments or scenarios. The template engine, powered by Go templating, abstracts away the boilerplate and repetitive YAML, promoting maintainability and reducing manual errors.

Another fundamental role of Helm is versioning and provenance tracking of deployments. By associating Charts with version numbers, Helm facilitates controlled application upgrades and rollbacks. This versioning capability integrates smoothly with GitOps workflows, where infrastructure as code (IaC) principles are enforced, further enhancing deployment reliability and auditability. Applications become tangible, versioned artifacts that can be shared internally or externally, fostering collaboration and governance.

Helm's functionality extends beyond mere templating; it automates the lifecycle management of Kubernetes applications. The Helm client interfaces with the Helm server-side component, known as Tiller (in Helm v2) or directly communicates with the Kubernetes API in Helm v3. Through this interaction, Helm orchestrates installation, upgrades, and uninstallation while monitoring release states. This abstraction simplifies operational complexity for DevOps teams and reduces the cognitive load required to manage Kubernetes resources manually.

Key use cases illustrate Helm's broad applicability:

- **Application Deployment and Upgrades**: Packaging applications with dependencies and handling versioned upgrades with minimal downtime.

- **Configuration Management**: Injecting environment-specific parameters systematically into deployments without duplicating manifests.

- **Microservices Management**: Coordinating interdependent services sharing common configuration or secrets.

- **CI/CD Pipeline Integration**: Automating deployment steps as part of build and release automation processes.

- **Repository and Artifact Management**: Hosting public or private Helm repositories to distribute and share application Charts across teams or organizations.

By consolidating deployment artifacts and automating the application lifecycle, Helm dramatically reduces complexity and risk associated with Kubernetes management. It enables organizations to transition from handcrafted, ad-hoc deployment processes to streamlined, repeatable, and auditable workflows, essential for scaling containerized applications in modern cloud-native environments.

Helm's inception addresses critical gaps in Kubernetes deployment practices by packaging and templating complex configurations, automating lifecycle management, and enhancing reproducibility through version control. Its role as the Kubernetes package manager empowers developers and operators alike to manage application complexity with efficiency and confidence, laying a foundation for modern cloud infrastructure automation.

1.4. Helm's Core Concepts and Terminology

Helm, as a package manager for Kubernetes, introduces a set of distinctive terms that form a structured vocabulary crucial for understanding its operation and deployment workflows. Mastering these terms is essential to grasp how Helm streamlines application deployment and management on Kubernetes clusters. The fundamental components include *charts, templates, releases, repositories*, and *values*. Each plays a unique role within the Helm architecture and the overall deployment lifecycle.

Charts serve as the primary packaging format in Helm. Conceptually, a chart is a collection of files that describe a related set of Kubernetes resources. Charts are versioned and shareable units of configuration, encapsulating the manifest files, necessary metadata, and templates required to deploy an application or service. Internally, a chart directory contains a mandatory Chart.yaml file, which specifies the chart's metadata such as name, version, description, and dependencies, accompanied by a templates directory that houses the manifest templates. Additionally, charts commonly include a values.yaml file that provides default configuration values to parameterize the templates.

Templates represent the dynamic aspect of charts. They are essentially Kubernetes manifest files coded in the Go templating language, allowing for parameter substitution and conditional logic. Templates enable reuse and customization by defining resource structures as blueprints rather than static manifests. During chart installation or upgrade, Helm renders these templates into concrete Kubernetes manifests by replacing variables and expressions with supplied configuration values. This templating mechanism facilitates flexible deployments, accommodating differences across environments without duplicating manifest files.

The **values** concept is pivotal to Helm's configurability. Values are structured data, typically written in YAML, that provide input parameters to the chart templates. The default values reside in the chart's values.yaml file, but these can be overridden or augmented at deployment time through command-line flags, external values files, or programmatically via Helm's APIs. This enables operators or automated systems to customize chart behavior precisely, such as specifying image tags, resource limits, replica counts, or feature flags. The values interface acts as a contract between the chart author and user that regulates which parameters are configurable.

Releases are instances of a chart deployed onto a Kubernetes cluster. Installing a chart with Helm creates a release-an encapsulation of the deployed resources, configuration values used, and metadata about deployment history. Each release is uniquely identified by a name within a namespace, enabling multiple deployments of the same chart with differing configurations or purposes. Helm maintains release records in the cluster, facilitating operations like upgrades, rollbacks, and uninstalls. Management of release life-cycles is a core Helm functionality that abstracts Kubernetes resource complexities into a single entity.

Repositories function as Helm's distribution mechanism. A Helm repository is a remote HTTP server hosting packaged charts, structured in an index format that Helm can query to locate and download charts. Common Helm repositories include public registries such as the Artifact Hub or custom corporate repositories. A repository stores packages in the form of compressed archives (tars) containing chart files and metadata, enabling easy sharing and versioning of applications. Helm provides commands to add, update, and search repositories, integrating seamlessly with the chart installation process.

Together, these components drive the Helm deployment pipeline. This pipeline begins with the acquisition of a chart from a repository, using the `helm install` command. Helm retrieves the chart package and merges the default `values.yaml` file with any user-supplied overrides. It then processes the templates by rendering Kubernetes manifests with the combined values. Finally, Helm applies these manifests to the Kubernetes cluster, creating or updating resources tracked as a release. The release metadata is stored within the cluster, enabling Helm's lifecycle management capabilities such as upgrades (`helm upgrade`), rollbacks (`helm rollback`), and uninstalls (`helm uninstall`).

The interplay of these terms also supports advanced features. For example, *dependencies* within charts allow composition of complex applications by referencing other charts. Charts can be versioned and maintained independently yet deployed together in a cohesive fashion. The `values.yaml` structure supports hierarchical overrides and can be centrally managed for consistent configuration across environments. The templating engine enables conditional resource creation, looping constructs, and customized output formats, all driven by the defined values.

Helm's vocabulary forms an interconnected ecosystem: *charts* encapsulate templates and values; *templates* define reusable manifest designs; *values* parameterize those templates; *releases* represent deployed chart instances; and *repositories* provide accessible storage and distribution. Understanding this terminology is the foundation of leveraging Helm's capabilities to automate and simplify Kubernetes application deployments efficiently and reliably.

1.5. Helm Client and Server Model: Evolution and Internals

Helm, as a package manager for Kubernetes, has undergone a fundamental architectural transformation from its initial releases to its current form. This evolution centers on the client-server interaction model that defines how Helm operates within a Kubernetes cluster. The original Helm 2 architecture employed a server-side component known as Tiller, which managed the deployment lifecycle of charts within the cluster. Helm 3 dispensed with Tiller, transitioning to a purely client-side architecture. This section deconstructs these models, elucidating the implications for security, performance, and operational workflows.

In Helm 2, the architecture was bifurcated into a CLI client and a server daemon running inside the Kubernetes cluster: Tiller. The Helm client was responsible for packaging, templating, and interacting with Tiller, which, in turn, executed actions against the Kubernetes API. Tiller maintained release state information in the cluster and handled the orchestration of charts, including installation, upgrade, and rollback. This design simplified certain operational aspects by centralizing release management but introduced notable security challenges.

Tiller operated with cluster-wide permissions to manage Kubernetes resources on behalf of users. It required Role-Based Access Control (RBAC) policies that, if improperly configured, risked privilege escalation or unauthorized modifications. The server-side nature also necessitated securing the communication channel between the Helm client and Tiller, which originally was not encrypted, potentially exposing sensitive information or commands. Despite its capabilities, Tiller's broad access posed a substantial attack surface, complicating security audits and regulatory compliance.

Operationally, Tiller introduced complexity in multi-tenant clusters. Different teams sharing a Kubernetes environment had to rely on sophisticated RBAC policies to isolate Helm releases. Additionally, Tiller's stateful design meant that loss or corruption of the Tiller pod could disrupt release management. Upgrading or scaling the Tiller deployment also required careful orchestration, as it represented a critical mid-layer in the Helm ecosystem.

The transition to Helm 3 marked a paradigm shift by removing Tiller entirely. The Helm client became the sole agent interacting directly with the Kubernetes API server, leveraging standard Kubernetes authentication and authorization mechanisms. This client-only approach eliminated the need for an additional in-cluster server, significantly simplifying the Helm architecture and improving security posture.

With no Tiller, Helm 3 performs all release management client-side, storing release metadata as Kubernetes secrets within the cluster's namespace. By relying on Kubernetes' native RBAC framework, Helm 3 enforces permissions consistently alongside other Kubernetes operations. This tightly integrates Helm into Kubernetes' security model, effectively reducing attack surface and aligning with principles of least privilege. The direct use of TLS-secured Kubernetes API communication ensures confidentiality and integrity of commands and data.

From a performance perspective, Helm 3 benefits from removing the overhead of an intermediary server. Commands are executed with fewer network hops, and Helm's stateless client model improves resilience and fault tolerance-there is no server state to maintain or recover. This simplification streamlines upgrades and operational maintenance. Users no longer need to manage an additional in-cluster component or complex RBAC policies specific to Tiller.

Operational workflows also shifted with Helm 3. The removal of Tiller means Helm releases are now fully namespaced and aligned with Kubernetes resource scoping. This enables more intuitive multi-tenancy and finer control over resource ownership. Developers and operators interact with Helm as a Kubernetes-native tool, reducing cognitive load and integration complexity. Tooling for CI/CD pipelines and audit logging benefits from Helm's alignment with standard Kubernetes APIs and access control.

While Helm 3's architecture offers improved security and operational simplicity, it imposes some new considerations. Since all release state is stored in Kubernetes secrets, namespace-level permissions must be granted carefully to prevent unauthorized access or tampering. Additionally, users must manage kubeconfig credentials and cluster access correctly, as Helm leverages these directly. However, these concerns are mitigated by Kubernetes' mature security ecosystem and Helm's adherence to its best practices.

Helm's architectural evolution from the Helm 2 client-server model with Tiller to the Helm 3 client-only model represents a critical enhancement in security, performance, and operational efficiency. The removal of Tiller closes attack vectors associated with cluster-wide privileged components and integrates Helm more tightly with Kubernetes' native RBAC and authentication mechanisms. Performance improvements stem from reduced communication layers and the stateless nature of the Helm client. Operationally, the simplification aligns Helm usage with Kubernetes conventions, facilitating better multi-tenancy and management workflows. This evolution underscores a broader trend in cloud-native tooling toward minimal privileged components and seamless integration with underlying orchestration frameworks.

1.6. Comparing Helm with Other Kubernetes Package Managers

Kubernetes package management has evolved to encompass a diversity of tools, each addressing specific deployment and configuration challenges in cloud-native environments. While Helm is widely regarded as the de facto standard for Kubernetes package management, alternative approaches such as Kustomize, Kapp, and Operators have gained traction, reflecting distinct design philosophies and use cases. This section presents an analytical comparison of these notable alternatives, illuminating the factors contributing to Helm's broad adoption and dominance.

Kustomize, introduced as a native Kubernetes configuration customization tool, diverges from Helm by eschewing templating in favor of a layered, patch-based approach. Configuration is managed through a base resource definition augmented by overlays that declaratively modify or extend these resources. This structure enables environment-specific tailoring without requiring a templating language. Kustomize's integration into the `kubectl` command-line tool simplifies adoption by obviating separate installation, thus offering a lightweight, native alternative. However, Kustomize primarily focuses on configuration management rather than packaging or dependency resolution. Complex dependency management is typically manual or must be orchestrated externally. Helm's templating and chart ecosystem, conversely, provides rich mechanisms for parameterization and dependency tracking through explicit chart metadata, facilitating widely reusable, shareable, and composable application packages.

Kapp (Kubernetes Application Package) is a tool from the Cloud Foundry ecosystem that emphasizes declarative lifecycle management and reconciliation of application resources. Unlike Helm's imperative install/upgrade/delete commands, Kapp continuously monitors resource state convergence against an explicit desired state definition, ensuring consistency and reducing configuration drift. Kapp also includes robust change detection and rollout strategies with detailed status reporting. Despite these strengths, Kapp intentionally limits its scope to deployment orchestration and does not incorporate templating or package templating akin to Helm charts. This positions Kapp as complementary in scenarios demanding tight operational control and observability of deployed resources, rather than as a broad package manager with rich ecosystem support.

Operators present a fundamentally different paradigm, encapsulating operational knowledge in Kubernetes-native controllers that automate application lifecycle tasks including installation, scaling, upgrading, backup, and failure recovery. Operators extend Kubernetes custom resource definitions (CRDs) with controllers encoding domain-specific logic, enabling complex stateful applications to be managed programmatically. While Helm packages deploy applications declaratively with configuration abstraction, Operators provide dynamic, event-driven management tailored to specific application behaviors. Operator frameworks such as Operator SDK facilitate development; however, Operators require significant investment in custom controller development and maintenance. Helm's extensive chart repository and simpler deployment model make it more accessible for general-purpose application packaging, especially for stateless or less operationally complex workloads. Nonetheless, Operators excel in scenarios demanding deep application-specific automation and tightly coupled lifecycle management.

Helm's distinctive advantages arise from its design as a full-fledged package manager, combining flexible templating with declarative configuration and automated dependency resolution. Helm charts abstract Kubernetes resource definitions through the Go templating engine, enabling parameter-driven customization while preserving underlying manifests' structure. Chart repositories, akin to traditional package registries, facilitate versioned, reusable distributions of applications and components. The Helm client-server architecture, maintained even as Helm v3 consolidated into a client-only model, supports straightforward installation, rollback, and upgrade workflows. Helm's ubiquity is reinforced by an extensive ecosystem of publicly available charts, broad community support, and compatibility with various CI/CD pipelines and GitOps tools.

In contrast, alternatives present significant concessions in either usability or functionality scope. Kustomize excels at simple, overlay-based environment customization, with minimal dependencies, but lacks Helm's abstraction and packaging richness. Kapp provides superior deployment state reconciliation and operational observability but omits chart packaging and templating capabilities. Operators offer unmatched automation for complex applications but demand substantial development effort and are specialized rather than general-purpose.

Helm's dominance can thus be attributed to its comprehensive feature set, balancing ease of use, flexibility, and composability across diverse application scenarios. Its templating paradigm, combined with a rich chart ecosystem, supports rapid, repeatable deployments at scale. However, practitioners often integrate Helm with complementary tools, deploying Kustomize overlays for environment-specific patches or adopting Operators for managing complex, stateful workloads. This hybrid approach leverages the strengths of each technology, enhancing Kubernetes application delivery and operations.

In operational environments, the choice among these tools frequently reflects project requirements: the complexity of application lifecycle automation, the need for environment-specific customization, operational monitoring priorities, and team expertise. Helm remains a foundational element in Kubernetes package management, particularly for stateless microservices and modular components. For sophisticated operational control and automation, Kapp and Operators provide valuable augmentations or alternatives. Kustomize fits best where simplicity and native support are paramount without extensive packaging needs.

This comparative landscape underscores the importance of understanding each tool's capabilities in relation to workload demands, operational maturity, and deployment consistency objectives. Helm's ongoing evolution and ecosystem maturity sustain its central role, even as complementary alternatives proliferate and mature, each carving specific niches in the Kubernetes application deployment and management spectrum.

Chapter 2

Crafting Helm Charts: Structure, Best Practices, and Lifecycle

Building robust and reusable Helm charts is both an art and a science—one that unlocks efficient, maintainable, and scalable deployments across environments. In this chapter, we go beyond boilerplate templates to unveil the engineering rigor and creative patterns underpinning effective chart design. Whether you're aiming to standardize deployments for a growing team or codify complex application lifecycles, you'll discover the subtle decisions and battle-tested techniques that separate fragile charts from enterprise-grade solutions.

2.1. Anatomy of a Helm Chart

A Helm chart serves as a packaged, reusable unit of a Kubernetes application, encapsulating all necessary resource definitions and configuration strategies within a defined directory structure. This modular structure is pivotal for managing complex, containerized deployments with flexibility, consistency, and scalability. Understanding the anatomy of a Helm chart requires a thorough examination of its core directories and files, which collectively orchestrate the deployment behavior.

At the root level of every Helm chart reside several key files and directories: `Chart.yaml`, `values.yaml`, the `templates` directory, and, optionally, the `charts` directory. Each component holds a distinctive role in defining and configuring the application.

Chart.yaml

The `Chart.yaml` file is the manifest descriptor of the Helm chart. Written in YAML format, it contains metadata about the chart, including its name, version, description, APIs it may depend on, and information relevant to Helm and Kubernetes versions compatibility. This file's primary purpose is to uniquely identify the chart and provide Helm with the necessary contextual details to manage the chart lifecycle, upgrades, and dependencies.

A minimal example of `Chart.yaml` might look like:

```
apiVersion: v2
name: my-application
description: A Helm chart for deploying My Application
type: application
version: 1.0.0
appVersion: 2.1.3
```

Here, `apiVersion` specifies the Helm chart API version, crucial for compatibility with Helm clients; `name` is the identifier for the chart; `version` relates to the chart's own versioning, distinct from the `appVersion`, which signifies the underlying application's version.

26

The `description` provides a brief narrative facilitating maintainability and discoverability in repositories.

values.yaml

Configuration flexibility is enabled primarily through the `values.yaml` file. This file defines default configuration values, acting as the primary repository of user-customizable parameters. When deploying an application, Helm merges these default values with user-provided overrides, be it via CLI `--set` flags or custom YAML files, to dynamically configure Kubernetes manifests.

The structure of `values.yaml` mirrors the expected configuration schema of the application, often hierarchically arranged to represent nested components and settings. For instance, replica counts, image repository tags, resource limits, and environment variables are frequently defined here.

An extract from `values.yaml` illustrating typical parameters:

```
replicaCount: 3

image:
  repository: myrepo/myapp
  tag: v2.1.3
  pullPolicy: IfNotPresent

service:
  type: ClusterIP
  port: 80

resources:
  limits:
    cpu: 100m
    memory: 128Mi
  requests:
    cpu: 100m
    memory: 64Mi
```

The separation provided by `values.yaml` is critical to maintain separation of concerns, enabling chart developers to set sensible defaults, while operators and DevOps engineers tailor deployments according to environment-specific needs without altering templated manifests directly.

templates Directory

At the core of a Helm chart's functionality lies the `templates` directory. This folder contains Kubernetes manifests written in YAML,
augmented by Go templating expressions and functions that allow
dynamic parameterization. These templates translate the static
structure into fully customized Kubernetes resource definitions at
deployment time, informed by values from `values.yaml` or user
overrides.

Common resource templates found here include:

- `deployment.yaml` – defines Deployment controllers managing application pods.

- `service.yaml` – describes Service objects exposing pods internally or externally.

- `ingress.yaml` – configures Ingress resources for HTTP and
  HTTPS routing.

- `configmap.yaml`, `secret.yaml` – manage configuration data
  and secrets.

Templates leverage Helm's templating language enabling conditional logic, loops, and function calls-for example, to selectively enable features or compute resource names. The templating engine
resolves these templates by interpolating values from the deployment context, producing valid Kubernetes manifests.

An abridged example snippet from a template file:

```
apiVersion: apps/v1
kind: Deployment
metadata:
  name: {{ .Release.Name }}-app
  labels:
    app.kubernetes.io/name: {{ .Chart.Name }}
    app.kubernetes.io/version: {{ .Chart.AppVersion }}
spec:
  replicas: {{ .Values.replicaCount }}
  selector:
```

```
    matchLabels:
      app.kubernetes.io/name: {{ .Chart.Name }}
  template:
    metadata:
      labels:
        app.kubernetes.io/name: {{ .Chart.Name }}
    spec:
      containers:
      - name: {{ .Chart.Name }}
        image: "{{ .Values.image.repository }}:{{ .Values.image.
    tag }}"
        imagePullPolicy: {{ .Values.image.pullPolicy }}
        resources:
          limits:
            cpu: {{ .Values.resources.limits.cpu }}
            memory: {{ .Values.resources.limits.memory }}
          requests:
            cpu: {{ .Values.resources.requests.cpu }}
            memory: {{ .Values.resources.requests.memory }}
```

This construct highlights how templating bridges variable deployment parameters with static manifest structure, ensuring both reuse and consistency across environments.

charts Directory

The charts directory is a container for chart dependencies packaged as Helm charts themselves. This design facilitates the modularization of complex applications by embedding subordinate charts-referred to as subcharts-within a parent chart. These subcharts represent reusable components or services that can be composed to form a larger system.

Chart dependencies are declared in Chart.yaml under the dependencies key with associated metadata such as repository URLs, version constraints, and weight preferences. When downloaded or packaged, these dependencies reside within the charts directory, allowing Helm to manage nested installations coherently.

This mechanism enables separation of concerns, where generic components (e.g., databases, caches) are maintained independently but can be version-controlled and updated alongside the primary application chart.

Interoperation and Lifecycle

The synergy between these components defines the Helm chart life-cycle stages:

- Metadata in `Chart.yaml` informs Helm about the chart identity and dependencies.

- Default configurations originate from `values.yaml`, providing deployment parameters.

- Templates in `templates` are dynamically rendered by substituting values into Kubernetes resource definitions.

- Dependencies nested under `charts` are recursively processed, integrating required components.

Upon installation, Helm combines static manifests with runtime-supplied configurations, validates Kubernetes API versions, and submits manifests to the cluster. Updates or rollbacks employ the same structure with versioned modifications to `values.yaml` or chart revisions.

The compartmentalized structure of Helm charts assures maintainability, extensibility, and clarity by delineating descriptive metadata, configurable parameters, manifest templates, and dependencies. Together, this anatomy constitutes a robust framework for delivering declarative, repeatable, and scalable Kubernetes applications.

2.2. Metadata and Versioning Strategies

In the context of Helm charts, metadata encapsulated within the `Chart.yaml` file plays a pivotal role in defining the identity, compatibility, and lifecycle management of a chart. This metadata not only guides Helm in installation and upgrade processes but also allows consumers of the chart to programmatically ascertain characteristics such as stability, compatibility, and lineage. Equally critical is the adoption of a robust versioning strategy grounded in semantic versioning (SemVer) principles, ensuring consistency and predictability during chart evolution, especially in complex deployment environments.

The `Chart.yaml` file is a YAML-encoded manifest describing the chart's metadata. Essential fields include:

- `name`: This uniquely identifies the chart within a repository. Naming conventions generally adhere to DNS label requirements to ensure broad compatibility.

- `version`: Denotes the chart's version following SemVer guidelines. This field is the primary means for consumers to determine upgrade eligibility.

- `appVersion`: Specifies the version of the underlying application that the chart deploys, separate from the chart's version. This distinction allows parallel evolution of the packaging and the application itself.

- `apiVersion`: Indicates the version of the chart API, guiding the Helm client on how to process the chart metadata.

- `description`: Provides a human-readable overview of the chart's purpose.

- `keywords`, `home`, `sources`, and `maintainers`: These fields enrich the chart's documentation and traceability but have less impact on versioning semantics.

- `dependencies`: Specifies other charts required for this chart to function, organized with version constraints and repository references.

31

Semantic Versioning (SemVer) is adopted almost universally for Helm charts, structured as `MAJOR.MINOR.PATCH`. The principles underlying SemVer directly influence how Helm performs upgrades and manages backward compatibility:

- **MAJOR** version increments signal incompatible API changes or breaking upgrades. When incremented, consumers must prepare for potentially significant manual intervention.

- **MINOR** version increments indicate the addition of functionality in a backward-compatible manner. Upgrades within a minor version series should not disrupt existing deployments.

- **PATCH** version increments reflect backward-compatible bug fixes or small changes that do not affect the chart's external interface.

Strict adherence to semantic versioning conventions enables Helm to leverage its built-in upgrade mechanisms safely, mitigating the risk of unexpected downtime or configuration drift.

The management of `dependencies` in `Chart.yaml` warrants particular attention. Dependency specifications follow this general format:

```
dependencies:
  - name: redis
    version: ">=10.0.0 <11.0.0"
    repository: "https://charts.bitnami.com/bitnami"
```

This indicates that the chart depends on any version within the 10.x series of Redis charts from a specified repository. Using semantic versioning constraints here is critical to maintaining compatibility without locking onto a single fixed version that might obstruct upgrades or cause conflicts.

Version constraints are typically expressed with operators such as

=, >, >=, <, <= and allow combinations that specify ranges. The specificity of these constraints must balance flexibility against the need for stability. Overly broad ranges risk dependency conflicts, while excessively restrictive constraints can cause Helm to fail to resolve a chart installation due to incompatible versions.

Upgrading charts without breaking consumers requires practices that both chart authors and users must observe. Authors should ensure that:

- Each release increment aligns strictly with SemVer rules, prominently updating the `version` field in `Chart.yaml`.

- Backward-incompatible changes (MAJOR version increments) are communicated clearly in changelogs and documentation.

- `appVersion` is updated independently to reflect changes in the underlying application, facilitating clarity for consumers tracking application-level upgrades.

- Dependency versions are carefully tested across supported version ranges to avoid introducing hidden incompatibilities.

- Deprecation notices are incorporated into chart defaults or documentation ahead of major breaking changes.

Consumers of charts should:

- Reference chart versions explicitly in their `requirements.yaml` or `Chart.yaml` dependencies section with version constraints that align with their risk tolerance.

- Monitor upstream changelogs and version bump semantics to anticipate necessary adaptations.

- Test upgrades in staging environments verifying that version transitions do not disrupt workloads.

An exemplary illustration of a carefully versioned Chart.yaml snippet adhering to these principles can be seen below:

```
apiVersion: v2
name: payment-service
description: A Helm chart for deploying the payment service
type: application
version: 2.1.3
appVersion: "3.4.5"
keywords:
  - payments
  - finance
  - service
dependencies:
  - name: database
    version: ">=5.0.0 <6.0.0"
    repository: "https://charts.example.com/databases"
maintainers:
  - name: Dev Team
    email: dev-team@example.com
```

By specifying version: 2.1.3, the chart indicates that this release is a patch update within the 2.1 minor series, thus guaranteeing API and behavior compatibility with prior 2.1.x releases. The appVersion is updated distinctly to reflect the deployed application version without implying packaging changes. The dependency on the database chart uses a range that permits any backward-compatible database update within the 5.x series.

Effective versioning paired with rich metadata in Chart.yaml thus forms the backbone of scalable, maintainable Helm chart ecosystems. It enables a transparent upgrade path and dependency framework where both chart authors and consumers can confidently manage deployments in complex environments without risking regressions or service disruptions.

2.3. Values Files and Hierarchical Configuration

Helm utilizes values.yaml files as the principal mechanism to externalize configuration parameters from chart templates, enabling adaptability and reusability across different environments. Harnessing the power of hierarchical configuration and overrides within these files is critical for managing dynamic deployments that span diverse environments without duplicating chart logic or compromising maintainability.

At its core, the `values.yaml` file provides a baseline set of key-value pairs that templates consume during rendering. However, when deploying to multiple environments, for example, development, staging, and production, rigid reliance on a single `values.yaml` becomes insufficient due to divergent configuration needs. To address this, Helm promotes a layered approach to configuration through the principle of inheritance and overlaying of values files.

Base and Environment-Specific Values Files

A common design pattern is to maintain one `values.yaml` as the base configuration, representing default settings suitable for most use cases. This base file contains keys for resource requests and limits, image tags, replica counts, service ports, and feature flags. To manage environment-specific adjustments, dedicated override files such as `values.dev.yaml`, `values.staging.yaml`, and `values.prod.yaml` are created. These overrides specify only the differences from the base, reducing duplication and making environment drift explicit.

For instance, consider a base `values.yaml` snippet:

```
replicaCount: 2
image:
  repository: myapp/backend
  tag: "1.0.0"
resources:
  requests:
    cpu: 100m
    memory: 128Mi
  limits:
    cpu: 200m
    memory: 256Mi
```

An override file for production `values.prod.yaml` might specify:

```
replicaCount: 5
image:
  tag: "1.0.0-prod"
resources:
  requests:
    cpu: 500m
    memory: 512Mi
  limits:
    cpu: 1
    memory: 1Gi
```

When deploying, Helm merges these files using the -f flag, layering values.prod.yaml on top of values.yaml. The effective value for replicaCount will therefore be 5, reflecting the override.

```
helm install myapp ./mychart -f values.yaml -f values.prod.yaml
```

Overrides and Merging Semantics

Helm performs a recursive merge of the YAML structures in values files. Scalar values are fully overridden by lower precedence files, whereas mapping types merge their keys, with child keys taking precedence over parents. This enables fine-grained overrides without the need to duplicate entire nested structures.

However, arrays (YAML sequences) behave differently: Helm's default merging strategy replaces an entire array rather than merging element-by-element. As a result, cautious design of configuration structures is essential to avoid unintended complete overwrites when multiple files are applied.

One technique to mitigate this is to encapsulate environment-dependent array modifications under distinct keys or to design configuration structures using maps rather than lists where possible, improving merge predictability.

Dynamic Configuration with Template Functions and Conditionals

While values.yaml files remain static YAML files, dynamic configuration is achievable within chart templates through Helm's tem-

36

plating language. Conditionals and functions allow rendering to adapt based on specific values.

For example, one can influence resource limits dynamically based on an environment variable or deployment stage:

```
resources:
  requests:
    cpu: {{ .Values.resources.requests.cpu | default "100m" }}
    memory: {{ .Values.resources.requests.memory | default "128Mi
      " }}
{{- if eq .Values.environment "production" }}
  limits:
    cpu: "1"
    memory: "1Gi"
{{- else }}
  limits:
    cpu: "200m"
    memory: "256Mi"
{{- end }}
```

By combining static values with templating logic, charts can react fluidly to environmental contexts while still benefiting from the structure and traceability values files afford.

Managing Complexity in Large-scale Deployments

As the number of environments and application components grows, it is common for configuration to become complex and unwieldy. Several practices are recommended to maintain clarity and control:

- Modularizing Values: Split configuration logically by feature or component into multiple files, then compose them via multiple -f flags in the desired order.

- Use of Helper Templates: Encapsulate recurrent conditional logic in named snippets within _helpers.tpl to avoid duplication in templates.

- Documentation and Conventions: Maintain clear documentation on which keys are environment-specific and what conventions govern overrides.

37

- Version Control Strategy: Track values files in version control, ideally in dedicated branches or directories per environment to facilitate audits and rollbacks.

- Validation and Linting: Leverage tooling, such as Helm's `lint` command and custom validation hooks, to catch misconfigurations early.

Advanced Patterns: Merging Values from External Sources

In large organizations, configurations may also need to be composed from external parameters originating in configuration management systems or secrets stores such as HashiCorp Vault, Consul, or Kubernetes ConfigMaps. While Helm itself does not natively integrate with these, a common pattern involves pre-processing values files or generating them dynamically during CI/CD pipelines.

For example, infrastructure tooling may generate environment-specific `values.generated.yaml` files from secret stores or templates, which are then layered last in Helm installs:

```
helm upgrade myapp ./mychart -f values.yaml -f values.prod.yaml -
    f values.generated.yaml
```

This approach enables secure, dynamic injection of sensitive or frequently changing configuration parameters while preserving the benefits of static base and override files for readability and versioning.

Summary of Best Practices

- Use a minimal base `values.yaml` as a starting point.

- Implement environment-specific overrides to isolate differences.

- Favor maps over arrays for better merge control.

38

- Combine values files with templating conditionals for flexibility.

- Modularize and document values structures to maintain oversight.

- Introduce automation to generate or validate values in complex pipelines.

Adhering to these principles ensures that Helm chart configurations remain adaptable, maintainable, and comprehensible across a wide range of deployment environments, thus empowering teams to manage Kubernetes applications at scale with confidence.

2.4. Templating with Go: Syntax and Advanced Directives

Go templating in Helm charts leverages the power of the Go `text/template` and `sprig` libraries to generate Kubernetes resource manifests dynamically, drastically reducing repetition and increasing flexibility. Mastery of this system requires a firm grasp of its syntax essentials, pipeline patterns, conditional logic, loops, and advanced directives to craft concise, maintainable, and DRY templates.

At the core of Go templating lies the use of delimiters {{ and }} to denote actions. Inside these delimiters, expressions can be variables, function calls, or control structures. The fundamental syntax form follows:

```
{{pipeline}}
```

where a *pipeline* represents a series of commands chained by the pipe operator |, with the output of one becoming the input of the next.

Pipelines and Variables

Pipelines facilitate composing complex expressions succinctly. A
pipeline can assign values to variables using the $ syntax, enabling
reuse and simplifying expressions:

```
{{- $name := .Values.name | default "default-name" -}}
metadata:
  name: {{ $name }}
```

Here, the variable $name stores the resolved resource name,
first attempting to extract .Values.name, and falling back to
"default-name" if none is provided. The dashes - control
whitespace trimming, promoting cleaner output.

Conditional Directives

Conditionals utilize if, else if, and else constructs to tailor manifest output based on values:

```
{{- if .Values.enabled }}
replicas: {{ .Values.replicas | default 1 }}
{{- else }}
replicas: 0
{{- end }}
```

This manipulation ensures components are only declared when explicitly enabled, embracing the DRY principle by omitting redundant definitions.

Iteration and Range

Loops, implemented via the range directive, traverse arrays, maps,
or slices:

```
{{- range $index, $port := .Values.ports }}
- name: port-{{ $index }}
  containerPort: {{ $port }}
{{- end }}
```

In this example, each port in .Values.ports is converted into a
container port specification with an index-generated name. Empty
arrays result in no output, preventing the need for additional conditional guards.

Built-in Functions and Sprig

The `sprig` library extends Go's basic function set, providing utilities for string manipulation, arithmetic, deep comparison, and list operations. Commonly used functions include `default`, `hasKey`, `pluck`, `b64enc`, and `quote`.

For instance:

```
{{- if hasKey .Values "configMapName" }}
name: {{ .Values.configMapName | quote }}
{{- end }}
```

Here, `hasKey` avoids runtime chart template errors by checking whether a key exists before dereferencing.

Complex Pipeline Usage

Chaining operations allows complex transformations inline:

```
{{- $image := printf "%s:%s" .Values.image.repository .Values.
    image.tag | quote -}}
image: {{ $image }}
```

This pipeline formats the `image` string by combining the repository and tag, then quotes it for YAML safety.

Nested Template Calls and Define Blocks

Templates encourage modularity via `define` and `template` keywords, enabling reusable snippets:

```
{{- define "mychart.labels" -}}
app: {{ .Chart.Name }}
chart: {{ .Chart.Name }}-{{ .Chart.Version | replace "+" "_" }}
{{- end }}

metadata:
  labels:
    {{- template "mychart.labels" . | nindent 4 }}
```

This approach encapsulates label generation logic, preventing duplication across multiple manifest files.

Conditional Rendering and Required Values

For critical parameters, the `required` function forces template execution failure if a value is missing:

```
image:
  repository: {{ required "Image repository is required!" .Values
    .image.repository }}
  tag: {{ .Values.image.tag | default "latest" }}
```

This technique enforces strong contract-like behavior for required configuration elements, improving chart robustness.

Whitespace Control and Comments

Fine control over output formatting is essential, especially to maintain valid YAML. Whitespace control uses minus signs – adjacent to delimiters:

```
{{- /* This comment will not add lines or spaces */ -}}
{{- if .Values.debug }}
debug: true
{{- end }}
```

Inline comments improve template readability without polluting the rendered manifest.

Error Handling and Debugging

Helm templates support error reporting with `fail` directive for custom validation failures:

```
{{- if and (.Values.enabled) (not .Values.requiredSetting) }}
{{ fail "requiredSetting must be set when enabled." }}
{{- end }}
```

Additionally, debugging can be accomplished via the `printf` function in combination with `fail` or temporary template outputs.

Best Practices

- Always use pipelines to enforce consistent, composable transformations.

- Prefer variables to reduce code repetition and enhance clarity.

- Employ `define` and `template` for reusable logic fragments.

- Use conditionals and range loops judiciously to create dynamic manifests that adapt to configuration inputs.

- Apply `required` for mandatory values to guarantee installation correctness.

- Control whitespace carefully to avoid syntax issues in generated YAML.

Mastering these aspects of Go templating within Helm charts results in flexible, maintainable Helm releases capable of adapting to diverse operational requirements while maintaining clear configuration semantics and manageable codebases.

2.5. Chart Dependencies and Subcharts

In Helm chart design, modularity and reuse are essential strategies for managing complexity and fostering maintainability in large-scale Kubernetes applications. These goals are achieved primarily through the use of *subcharts* and the `requirements.yaml` (or the more recent `Chart.yaml` dependencies field), which enable encapsulation of related resources, version control, and composability.

A **subchart** is a Helm chart nested inside another chart's `charts/` directory or specified as a dependency. It functions as an independent entity maintaining its own templates, values, and lifecycle, but it is deployed as part of the parent chart. This encapsulation allows teams to develop reusable components: for instance, a database, a cache layer, or a message broker can be packaged once and included as subcharts across multiple parent charts, avoiding duplication and easing upgrades.

The `requirements.yaml` file (deprecated in Helm 3 in favor of defining dependencies inside `Chart.yaml`) traditionally lists a chart's dependencies along with version constraints and

43

repository locations. This file instructs Helm to fetch and place
dependent charts into the `charts/` folder during chart building
and installation, thereby resolving and locking the complete
dependency tree. For Helm 3 and beyond, the dependency
management is articulated as follows inside `Chart.yaml`:

```
dependencies:
  - name: redis
    version: 14.4.0
    repository: "https://charts.bitnami.com/bitnami"
  - name: postgresql
    version: 9.6.2
    repository: "https://charts.bitnami.com/bitnami"
```

Defining dependencies with precise version locks is critical to guaranteeing consistent and repeatable deployments, especially across
multiple environments or clusters. Helm adheres to semantic versioning for dependency resolution and alerts when conflicts occur,
enabling controlled upgrades and rollbacks within your application ecosystem.

Managing shared resources requires careful handling, as dependencies enable reuse but also introduce challenges in resource
sharing and configuration collision. Subcharts inherently isolate
their templates and values; however, the global namespace of Kubernetes resources requires careful naming and scoping to prevent
conflicts. Helm provides several mechanisms to mitigate these issues.

One key mechanism is the use of `.Values` overrides and value
merging. When a parent chart includes subcharts, it can override
values by creating a nested structure keyed by the subchart name:

```
redis:
  fullnameOverride: "myapp-redis"
  service:
    type: ClusterIP

postgresql:
  fullnameOverride: "myapp-postgres"
  persistence:
    enabled: true
```

This approach allows consistent customization and avoids hard-coding names inside subcharts, enhancing reusability and facilitating environment-specific adjustments. Additionally, subcharts can leverage the `.Release.Name` and `.Chart.Name` built-in template variables to generate unique resource names dynamically.

Another layer of control is provided through the `global` values section. Values defined under the `global` key in the parent chart propagate to all subcharts, enabling coordinated configuration of common parameters such as image repositories, logging levels, or security policies:

```
global:
  imagePullSecrets:
    - name: my-registry-secret
  commonLabels:
    app.kubernetes.io/managed-by: my-helm-controller
```

Subcharts use `.Values.global` access to read these values, ensuring that shared configurations remain consistently applied throughout the dependency hierarchy.

For extensive applications composed of numerous subcharts, understanding and managing the dependency tree becomes a nuanced challenge. Helm resolves dependencies recursively: each subchart may declare its own subdependencies, resulting in a potentially deep and wide dependency graph.

Key behaviors and considerations include:

- **Flattening dependencies during packaging**: Helm flattens the dependency tree into the `charts/` directory during packaging, importing all required charts to a single directory for installation. This flattening simplifies Helm's internal processing but necessitates that all dependencies are compatible and do not conflict.

- **Version conflicts and resolution**: When different subcharts depend on varying versions of the same chart, Helm attempts best-effort resolution but may require manual intervention or explicit overrides. Careful dependency version management and alignment across the ecosystem are vital to avoid deployment failures or inconsistent environments.

- **Shared resource deduplication**: Multiple subcharts referencing common base charts (e.g., the same database chart) can unintentionally deploy redundant resources if not carefully configured. Using the `global` values pattern or designing subcharts to be "library charts" - which provide reusable templates but do not deploy resources by themselves - can alleviate duplication.

- **Lifecycle considerations**: When uninstalling a parent chart, dependencies are typically uninstalled as well. However, for subcharts used independently or shared across different parent charts, explicit considerations on retention or upgrades must be managed, often through hooks or custom lifecycle policies.

- **Debugging and visualization**: Helm offers commands such as `helm dependency build`, `helm dependency update`, and `helm dependency list` to manage dependencies. Visualizing the dependency graph externally or using supplementary tools improves understanding in complex deployments.

Effective modular chart design leverages subcharts and dependencies to maximize reuse while minimizing friction:

- **Design subcharts as standalone, self-contained units** with clear interfaces and minimal assumptions about the parent environment.

- **Promote value overrides and** `global` **values** for tunable parameters, enabling centralized control.

- **Use distinct naming conventions and templates** to avoid resource conflicts, taking advantage of Helm's templating and predefined variables.

- **Define precise version constraints** to ensure compatibility and reproducibility.

- **Document dependency trees and intended configurations** explicitly to prevent confusion during collaboration and upgrades.

In complex applications, the discipline of chart dependency management transforms into an architecture pattern, akin to software package management, rather than merely a templating convenience. Mastering these nuances enables sustainable and scalable Helm chart ecosystems suited to enterprise-grade Kubernetes deployments.

2.6. Lifecycle Hooks and Advanced Chart Events

Helm's lifecycle hooks provide a powerful mechanism for embedding custom logic at precise moments in the lifecycle of chart deployment. These hooks-such as `pre-install`, `post-install`, `pre-delete`, `post-delete`, and `test`-enable sophisticated orchestration and automation beyond simple resource templating. By integrating Helm hooks into charts, operators can coordinate ancillary tasks, validate deployments, and manage complex dependencies with finer control.

A Helm hook is declared by annotating Kubernetes manifest resources within a chart with the `"helm.sh/hook"` annotation. This instructs Helm to intercept the normal lifecycle flow, running the annotated resource at the specified hook event instead of immediately applying it as part of the primary installation or upgrade.

For example, a `pre-install` hook is executed before the main installation begins, allowing preparatory logic or configuration to be deployed or validated first.

The core Helm lifecycle hooks include:

- **pre-install**: Executes before any resources defined in the chart manifest are installed.

- **post-install**: Runs after all regular chart resources have been installed successfully.

- **pre-delete**: Runs before any resources in the chart are deleted.

- **post-delete**: Executes after all resources in the chart have been removed.

- **pre-upgrade** and **post-upgrade**: Run respectively before and after chart upgrades.

- **test**: Used to run diagnostic or validation pods to verify the deployment.

Each hook can execute arbitrary Kubernetes resources, but jobs are most commonly used due to their ephemeral execution and explicit success/failure reporting semantics. When a hook job runs, Helm tracks its completion state. If the job fails or times out, the Helm release can be marked accordingly, allowing for automated remediation or rollback.

A typical example of a `pre-install` hook might be a Job that performs prerequisite validation of external dependencies or initializes an external database schema. The following snippet shows a Job manifest annotated as a pre-install hook:

```
apiVersion: batch/v1
kind: Job
metadata:
  name: validate-external-service
```

```
  annotations:
    "helm.sh/hook": pre-install
spec:
  template:
    spec:
      containers:
      - name: validator
        image: myregistry/external-validator:latest
        command: ["./validate.sh"]
      restartPolicy: OnFailure
```

Upon running `helm install`, Helm schedules the `validate-external-service` job before installing the remaining chart resources. Success of this job is a gatekeeper for the installation workflow.

Advanced usage often leverages multiple hooks in the same chart, complementing orchestration workflows. For instance, a `post-install` hook might trigger data migration jobs immediately after the main services are deployed but before they become fully available. This intermixed execution turns Helm into a lightweight workflow engine capable of managing lifecycle-dependent tasks.

Helm also allows fine-grained control over hook execution order and failure policies through additional annotations:

- `helm.sh/hook-weight`: An integer annotation that dictates execution order relative to other hooks of the same type; lower weights run first.

- `helm.sh/hook-delete-policy`: Controls when and if hook resources are deleted, with options like `hook-succeeded`, `hook-failed`, or `before-hook-creation`.

- `helm.sh/hook-timeout`: Specifies a timeout for hook execution in seconds.

The weighting mechanism is instrumental when multiple hooks of a given event must run in sequence. For example, a `pre-install`

hook with weight 0 can validate environment variables, while one
with weight 10 might perform auxiliary setup. Helm honors these
weights and executes hooks according to ascending weights.

Consider the following annotated Job manifest fragment demonstrating some of these advanced annotations:

```
metadata:
  annotations:
    "helm.sh/hook": post-install
    "helm.sh/hook-weight": "5"
    "helm.sh/hook-delete-policy": hook-succeeded
    "helm.sh/hook-timeout": "300"
```

This ensures that the post-install hook runs with priority 5, is
cleaned up immediately after a successful run, and fails if it does
not complete within 5 minutes.

The test hook type is specialized for deploying diagnostic workloads against the currently deployed release. Helm's helm test
command triggers these test pods, helping operators automate
health checks or compliance verifications as part of continuous
deployment pipelines. A test job typically contains assertions or
probes against the deployed system and returns success only if all
checks pass.

Handling failures in hooks requires careful design. By default,
Helm will abort an installation or upgrade operation if a hook
fails. However, the hook-delete-policy and retry logic embodied
within Kubernetes Jobs provide options to recover or rerun hooks
as needed. Furthermore, hooks do not create resources that remain part of the release's primary manifest, which means any long-
running service or persistent resource should not be deployed as a
hook.

From a security perspective, hooks run with the same privileges as
regular pods within the release and should observe the principle of
least privilege. Ensure image sources are trusted and commands
executed in hooks are idempotent since retries may occur during
failure.

In complex deployment scenarios-such as managing migrations, integration with external cloud services, or custom initialization workflows-employing Helm lifecycle hooks becomes indispensable for implementing reliable and repeatable automation. Their integration tightly couples custom logic to chart deployment semantics, transforming Helm charts from static resource collections into dynamic, orchestrated application lifecycles.

The correct orchestration of hooks can alleviate problems like race conditions between dependent resources, manual intervention in deployment phases, or inconsistent validation states. Helm's powerful lifecycle event model thus extends Kubernetes deployment capabilities significantly, fostering automation practices essential for modern infrastructure as code methodologies.

2.7. Reusable Templates and Chart Library Patterns

Achieving maintainable and scalable deployment architectures for infrastructure-as-code representations hinges on modularity and reuse of template components. This principle is especially critical when managing multiple Kubernetes Helm charts or similar packaging formats, where shared logic and configuration patterns frequently recur across diverse applications and environments. Reusable template partials, helper functions, and centralized chart libraries collectively enable the systematic extraction, consolidation, and propagation of common logic, drastically reducing duplication risks and streamlining ongoing maintenance.

Fundamentally, template partials serve as building blocks-discrete, parameterized snippets encapsulating recurrent manifest segments or configuration constructs. By externalizing such segments into separate files, these partials can be independently versioned and referenced by multiple charts. Within Helm, for example, this is achieved by storing partials

under the `templates/` directory with a filename prefixed by an
underscore and invoking them via the {- `include` ... -} or {-
`template` ... -} directives.

The extraction of partials begins with identifying duplicated
YAML structures, such as container definitions, volume mounts,
or ingress rules, which differ only marginally by parameters.
Instead of redefining these fragments per chart, they become
parameterizable partials receiving values through the template
scope. This approach promotes DRY (Don't Repeat Yourself)
compliance and consolidates bug fixes and feature enhancements
into a single source of truth. Parameters passed to partials
may include primitive values, nested dictionaries, or even lists,
providing flexible control over rendering logic.

Complementing template partials is the systematic use of helper
functions-custom-defined Go template functions invoked inline or
within partials to perform common transformations, validations,
or string manipulations. Helpers act as micro-utilities supplying reusable procedural logic that enhances expressiveness without prematurely cluttering templates with duplication. For instance, functions that normalize label keys, sanitize input values,
or consolidate resource requests can be defined once under the
`_helpers.tpl` file and called uniformly across different manifests
or charts. Utilizing helpers not only reinforces consistency but
aids in abstracting chart-specific idiosyncrasies, simplifying both
authoring and review processes.

To orchestrate reuse on a broader scope, chart libraries encapsulate collections of reusable partials, helpers, and values, packaged as separate Helm charts without deployable resources. These
chart libraries can then be declared as dependencies in user-facing
charts' `Chart.yaml` files. By doing so, multiple consumer charts
seamlessly inherit the shared baseline configuration and template
functions, ensuring uniformity across an organization's portfolio.
Chart libraries promote centralized governance over operational

best practices-such as standardized security context definitions, resource limits, and monitoring annotations-while empowering users to override or extend these defaults as necessary.

Effective integration and management of shared logic via libraries require deliberate versioning strategies, semantic version control, and clear API boundaries akin to software library design. Rigid contracts must be maintained to prevent unexpected breaks downstream. Embedding comprehensive documentation and examples within library charts further accelerates adoption and reduces the learning curve for new chart maintainers.

An illustrative example demonstrates leveraging a chart library to render standardized pod metadata labels. The library defines a helper function encapsulating label construction logic:

```
{{/* Define labels helper in _helpers.tpl */}}
{{- define "common.labels" -}}
app.kubernetes.io/name: {{ .Chart.Name | quote }}
app.kubernetes.io/version: {{ .Chart.Version | quote }}
app.kubernetes.io/instance: {{ .Release.Name | quote }}
{{- end -}}
```

A consuming chart imports this library and invokes `"common.labels"` within its pod spec metadata:

```
metadata:
  labels:
    {{- include "common.labels" . | nindent 4 }}
```

Thus, any update to the labeling strategy requires a single modification inside the library, which then propagates automatically to all dependent charts upon dependency upgrades.

In addition to template and helper reuse within Helm, many modern chart ecosystems offer advanced capabilities like global values inheritance. This feature enables top-level configuration parameters defined in a global values file to cascade into all subcharts, enabling uniform control without redundant specification. Usage patterns encourage defining a `global` section in `values.yaml`, which libraries and charts query to shape default behaviors.

While chart libraries and partials contribute significantly to scalable chart development, they must be employed thoughtfully. Overly generic partials risk becoming opaque or overly complex, complicating template readability and troubleshooting. Balancing generality versus specificity is an art that depends on organizational scale and diversification of deployment targets. Strategy recommendations include limiting partial complexity, emphasizing well-documented interfaces, and promoting idiomatic naming conventions for helpers.

Other patterns enhancing reuse include:

- **Value Object Composition:** Breaking down values files into modular components that can be merged or overridden allows more granular reuse of configuration snippets.

- **Conditional Templates:** Leveraging conditionals extensively within templates to enable or disable features based on provided values minimizes needless code proliferation.

- **Test Harnesses:** Implementing automated rendering tests that exercise partials and helpers across scenarios ensures correctness and guards against regression during evolution.

The architecture of reusable templates and chart library patterns underpins maintainability and scalability in complex deployment environments. By rigorously extracting common logic into partials, codifying repeatable operations via helpers, and packaging these within version-controlled chart libraries, organizations achieve a robust foundation for consistent, efficient, and auditable container orchestration automation. This modular strategy not only accelerates development velocity but also fosters uniform compliance with security, operational, and performance standards, ultimately reducing technical debt and facilitating continuous improvement.

Chapter 3

Advanced Templating and Value Management

Beyond basic variable substitution lies a powerful realm of advanced templating and value management—where Helm charts become not just configurable, but truly intelligent. This chapter uncovers the hidden potential of Helm's template engine, revealing how complexity can be tamed with dynamic logic, data transformations, and rigorous validation. Prepare to elevate your charts from mere manifests to adaptable blueprints, engineered for reliability, testing, and automation at scale.

3.1. Conditional Logic and Flow Control

Helm templates leverage the Go template language to implement conditional logic and flow control, which are essential for creating flexible, parameterized Kubernetes manifests. Mastery of `if-else` statements, range loops, and branching constructs enables the deployment of dynamic resources, optional configuration features, and variant deployment paths. This section delves into these constructs with a focus on practical patterns, common pitfalls, and strategies to maintain templates that remain readable and scalable.

The fundamental control structure in Helm templates is the if-else conditional. It evaluates whether a given expression is true or false and selectively renders template fragments accordingly. For example, conditional inclusion of a sidecar container based on a user-defined value can be expressed as:

```
{{- if .Values.enableSidecar }}
  - name: sidecar
    image: {{ .Values.sidecarImage }}
{{- else }}
  # No sidecar container added
{{- end }}
```

The dash (–) after the opening and before the closing double braces suppresses extraneous whitespace, which is crucial to preserving valid YAML indentation. The if condition can evaluate any boolean expression, including comparisons, existence checks, and negations.

For scenarios requiring mutually exclusive conditions, Helm provides the else if syntax, allowing branching among multiple alternatives:

```
{{- if eq .Values.environment "prod" }}
replicas: 5
{{- else if eq .Values.environment "staging" }}
replicas: 3
{{- else }}
replicas: 1
{{- end }}
```

This pattern supports complex decision trees but should be applied judiciously to avoid deeply nested and intertwined logic.

Looping over collections of items is another core aspect of dynamic template generation. The `range` action iterates over arrays, slices, or maps. It is commonly used to create multiple resource entries or to parameterize container specifications:

```
containers:
{{- range .Values.containers }}
  - name: {{ .name }}
    image: {{ .image }}
    ports:
    {{- range .ports }}
      - containerPort: {{ . }}
    {{- end }}
{{- end }}
```

This nested `range` example demonstrates how Helm templates can iterate over a list of container definitions and their associated ports, enabling arbitrary container configurations defined through values.

Branching and looping, while powerful, can introduce maintenance challenges. Several anti-patterns frequently emerge in Helm templates, undermining clarity and extendibility:

- **Excessive Nesting:** Embedding multiple `if` and `range` statements within each other can lead to overly complex and difficult-to-follow templates. To mitigate this, break up template logic into smaller named templates using `define` and `template` commands, promoting modularity.

- **Heavy Logic in Templates:** Helm templates should focus on presentation and resource assembly, while business rules and complex validations reside in external value files or pre-processing steps. Overloading template logic increases the risk of subtle bugs and makes debugging harder.

- **Repeated Conditional Blocks:** Duplicating similar conditional blocks for slightly different resource definitions can be replaced by parameterized sub-templates or inclusion logic, reducing code duplication and easing future changes.

To maintain clear and manageable templates as complexity grows, architects often partition conditional logic by functionality into separate template files and use consistent indentation and whitespace management. A reliable pattern is to centralize feature toggles in the `values.yaml` file, preserving a single source of truth for conditional branches.

Parameterized deployment paths allow Helm charts to deploy significantly different configurations based on user-defined inputs. For instance, enabling persistent storage conditionally through parameters can be implemented as:

```
{{- if .Values.persistence.enabled }}
volumeMounts:
  - name: data
    mountPath: /var/lib/data
volumes:
  - name: data
    persistentVolumeClaim:
      claimName: {{ .Values.persistence.claimName }}
{{- end }}
```

This clear gating mechanism ensures resources related to stateful storage are only rendered if explicitly requested. Helm's capability to dynamically include or omit entire Kubernetes resources prevents unnecessary resource creation and reduces deployment footprint.

Another advanced use case is conditional resource generation based on the existence of parameters. For example, only generate an ingress resource when the ingress hostname is set:

```
{{- if .Values.ingress.hostname }}
apiVersion: networking.k8s.io/v1
kind: Ingress
metadata:
  name: {{ include "chart.fullname" . }}
spec:
  rules:
    - host: {{ .Values.ingress.hostname }}
      http:
        paths:
          - path: /
            pathType: Prefix
            backend:
              service:
```

```
                   name: {{ include "chart.fullname" . }}
                   port:
                     number: 80
{{- end }}
```

Failing to guard resource definitions with adequate conditional logic leads to partial or invalid manifests, which can cause Helm install or upgrade operations to fail.

Furthermore, Helm permits combining flow control constructs with built-in functions such as `default`, `hasKey`, and `required` to create robust validation and fallback pathways. The `required` function enforces that certain values must be set, ensuring template correctness prior to deployment:

```
{{- required "Error: service.port is required" .Values.service.
    port }}
```

Helm's conditional logic and flow control facilities empower chart developers to define adaptable, reusable templates that conform tightly to diverse deployment requirements. Employing `if-else` statements, `range` loops, and branching to selectively generate resources creates a declarative and expressive mechanism for managing Kubernetes manifests. Awareness of anti-patterns such as excessive nesting and heavy template logic is key to keeping complex flows maintainable. Modularizing logic and centralizing configuration parameters enhance template clarity, fostering scalability and ease of maintenance.

3.2. Complex Data Structures and Mapping in Helm

The `values.yaml` file serves as the cornerstone for configuration in Helm charts, enabling users to tailor chart behavior to a wide range of deployment environments. While simple key-value pairs suffice for basic configuration, more advanced scenarios demand the use of complex data structures such as lists, maps, and deeply

59

nested mappings. Proper utilization of these structures enhances modularity, maintainability, and reduces configuration errors.

Modeling lists in `values.yaml` enables the representation of ordered collections of values. They are essential when specifying multiple similar entities, such as node selectors, container environment variables, or network policies. A list is defined using a YAML dash syntax:

```
nodeSelectorLabels:
  - environment=prod
  - region=us-east
  - tier=backend
```

Within Helm templates, lists are iterated using the range directive:

```
{{- range .Values.nodeSelectorLabels }}
- {{ . }}
{{- end }}
```

When lists contain complex objects, each element can be a map, enabling intricate configurations. For example, modeling multiple containers with their respective ports is achieved as follows:

```
containers:
  - name: app
    image: myapp:1.0
    ports:
      - containerPort: 8080
  - name: sidecar
    image: sidecar:2.0
    ports:
      - containerPort: 9090
```

In templates, accessing nested list elements requires chaining range directives accordingly, mindful of scope to avoid overshadowing variables.

Maps represent unordered key-value pairs and are fundamental to representing configuration parameters that are naturally grouped. Unlike primitive key-value pairs, maps allow nested structures embodying hierarchical relationships.

Consider configuring ingress rules with nested maps:

60

```
ingress:
  enabled: true
  annotations:
    kubernetes.io/ingress.class: nginx
    cert-manager.io/cluster-issuer: "letsencrypt-prod"
  hosts:
    - host: example.com
      paths:
        - path: /
          pathType: Prefix
    - host: api.example.com
      paths:
        - path: /v1
          pathType: Prefix
```

The use of maps within lists (e.g., hosts containing paths) is common and requires careful template logic to navigate the hierarchy. Template expressions must explicitly address each level, preserving the context of parent nodes and avoiding key collisions.

As the complexity of values increases, deeply nested structures become prevalent. While powerful, they carry the risk of reduced readability and increased potential for misconfiguration. A balance between depth and clarity must be struck.

Structured indentation with meaningful keys is crucial. For example, when defining service configurations that encompass both network and resource specifications:

```
service:
  type: ClusterIP
  ports:
    http:
      port: 80
      targetPort: 8080
      protocol: TCP
    metrics:
      port: 9113
      targetPort: 9113
      protocol: TCP
  resources:
    limits:
      cpu: "500m"
      memory: "256Mi"
    requests:
      cpu: "250m"
      memory: "128Mi"
```

Here, logical grouping aids both human comprehension and programmatic access. When templates require access to such nested values, dot notation is used consistently:

```
.service.ports.http.port
.resources.limits.cpu
```

Helm templates should always validate the existence of nested keys to avoid runtime errors. The `default` function is effective for providing fallback values:

```
{{ .Values.service.ports.http.port | default 80 }}
```

A hierarchical structure with clear conceptual boundaries enhances both usability and extensibility. The following guidelines contribute to a resilient configuration design:

- **Consistent Naming Conventions**: Use descriptive and consistent keys to express the meaning and scope of each configuration parameter.

- **Avoid Excessive Nesting**: Deeply nested values should be limited to what is necessary; otherwise, refactor the configuration by splitting into logical subcharts or external files.

- **Document Structures Clearly**: Inline comments and accompanying documentation reduce misunderstandings and misconfigurations.

- **Use Defaults and Validation**: Employ default values within templates and, where possible, leverage Helm's `.Capabilities` or external validation tools to ensure value correctness before deployment.

- **Separate Concerns**: Differentiate between operational parameters (e.g., replica counts), environment-specific overrides, and sensitive or secrets management-often externalized via Kubernetes Secrets or Helm secrets plugins.

62

Handling complex maps and lists imposes challenges around data correctness and maintainability. Strategies to mitigate errors include:

- **Explicit Type Expectations**: Be explicit in Helm template logic regarding the expected data types. Use the `kindIs` function to validate types, preventing type mismatch errors.

- **Fail Fast in Templates**: When critical configuration is missing or malformed, use the `fail` function to halt rendering with meaningful diagnostics.

```
{{- if not .Values.service.ports }}
  {{ fail "service.ports must be defined" }}
{{- end }}
```

- **Template Reuse and Extraction**: Utilize named templates to encapsulate complex logic, reducing duplication and simplifying maintenance.

- **Automated Validation Pipelines**: Integrate tools like `helm lint`, YAML schema validators, or custom scripts to validate `values.yaml` structure prior to deployment.

Translating hierarchical Helm values into Kubernetes manifests involves navigating nested structures efficiently while maintaining readability and correctness. For instance, rendering environment variables from a complex list of maps:

```
env:
  - name: LOG_LEVEL
    value: DEBUG
  - name: ENABLE_FEATURE_X
    value: "true"
```

The template might appear as:

```
env:
{{- range .Values.env }}
  - name: {{ .name }}
    value: {{ .value | quote }}
{{- end }}
```

Such patterns generalize to other Kubernetes resources like annotations, labels, volume mounts, or network policies, which often require iterative rendering of list elements mapped from `values.yaml`.

Mastering complex data structures in Helm's `values.yaml` enables precise, scalable configuration management. It empowers chart authors and operators to express sophisticated deployment paradigms, ensuring consistency, reducing redundancy, and enhancing maintainability across diverse Kubernetes environments.

3.3. Advanced Sprig Functions and Custom Helper Functions

Helm charts rely heavily on templating capabilities to enable dynamic and flexible Kubernetes resource definitions. Sprig, a comprehensive library of Go template functions, significantly enhances these capabilities by providing a suite of versatile utilities for string manipulation, numeric operations, data transformation, and control flow. When combined with custom helper templates, Sprig functions empower chart developers to implement advanced logic and reusable components, thereby maintaining DRY principles and promoting maintainability.

Sprig functions can be categorized broadly into several domains: string and text processing, numeric and date utilities, collections handling, and cryptographic functions. One common use case involves string manipulation functions such as `trim`, `replace`, `lower`, `upper`, and `regexReplaceAll`, which enable dynamic formatting of input values or Kubernetes resource metadata. For instance, converting namespace names to lowercase for labeling consistency or sanitizing release names for use as container labels can be achieved succinctly with Sprig:

```
{{- $ns := .Release.Namespace | lower | trim }}
metadata:
  labels:
```

```
namespace: {{ $ns }}
```

Numeric operations extend beyond basic arithmetic; Sprig supplies functions like add, sub, mul, div, and mod, facilitating dynamic resource calculations within Helm templates. For example, you may compute resource requests programmatically based on input parameters:

```
resources:
  requests:
    cpu: "{{ mul .Values.cpuRequest 1000 }}m"
    memory: "{{ mul .Values.memoryRequest 1024 }}Mi"
```

Advanced temporal functions such as now, date, and dateInZone allow manipulation and formatting of timestamps, useful when generating annotations or labels that embed build or deployment dates.

Sprig's list and dictionary utilities include hasKey, pluck, tuple, and dict. These are indispensable when dealing with complex input values structured as maps or lists inside values.yaml. Efficient data extraction and reorganization enable templates that adapt based on user inputs, reducing hardcoded behavior.

Despite the robustness of Sprig, chart writers often encounter recurring patterns that benefit from encapsulation via custom helper functions. These helpers are defined as named templates within Helm's _helpers.tpl file and can include sophisticated control structures, parameterization, and recursive logic. Utilization of custom helpers modularizes the code, improves readability, and simplifies upgrades or debugging.

A common example is the normalization of resource names. To ensure compliance with Kubernetes naming conventions, helper templates can encapsulate multiple Sprig calls, such as trimming whitespace, converting to lowercase, and substituting invalid characters:

```
{{- define "mychart.normalizeName" -}}
{{- trim (regexReplaceAll "[^a-z0-9-]" (lower .)) "-" -}}
```

```
{{- end -}}
```

Usage inside templates then calls this helper with a parameter:

```
metadata:
  name: {{ include "mychart.normalizeName" .Release.Name }}
```

Another powerful use of custom helpers is implementing conditional logic that cannot be easily expressed inline. For example, creating a helper to select image tags based on input flags or environment variables provides clarity and prevents duplication:

```
{{- define "mychart.selectImageTag" -}}
{{- if .Values.app.image.tagOverride -}}
{{- .Values.app.image.tagOverride -}}
{{- else -}}
{{- if eq .Values.env "production" -}}
"stable"
{{- else -}}
"latest"
{{- end -}}
{{- end -}}
{{- end -}}
```

This helper can be incorporated seamlessly:

```
image:
  repository: {{ .Values.app.image.repository }}
  tag: {{ include "mychart.selectImageTag" . }}
```

Recursive helpers further extend Helm's expressivity. For instance, when processing arbitrarily deep nested configuration maps, a recursive template can serialize key-value pairs into flat lists or perform conditional transformations. This approach avoids manual unrolling of complex data structures, preserving genericity.

Moreover, the combination of Sprig's cryptographic functions such as sha1, sha256, and b64enc allows secure hashing or encoding of values within templates. Integrating such functions into custom helpers supports unique naming, cache busting, or validation logic tied to content fingerprints.

Advanced Sprig functions and custom helper templates collectively enable a Helm chart to behave like a domain-specific language, capable of abstracting intricacies of Kubernetes manifests while offering extensibility and dynamic behavior. By judiciously leveraging these techniques, chart maintainers can minimize template bloat, enforce conventions centrally, and provide intuitive interfaces for users.

Mastering Sprig's full function library and designing comprehensive helper templates elevates Helm chart authoring from mere templating to sophisticated programmatic resource generation, vital for complex deployment scenarios and scalable infrastructure as code workflows.

3.4. Parameterization and Externalizing Configuration

Effective parameterization and the externalization of configuration are foundational for managing complex deployments within Helm charts, particularly as applications scale and compose into sophisticated hierarchies of charts and subcharts. Passing parameters cleanly and flexibly across multiple chart levels ensures maintainability, avoids duplication, and enhances reusability. This section analyzes established patterns for parameter propagation and demonstrates methods to inject values from environment variables, CI/CD pipelines, and other external sources, thus maximizing the agility and adaptability of deployment workflows.

Helm charts are often organized in layered structures, where a parent chart incorporates multiple subcharts, each potentially requiring customized values. Directly embedding all subchart-specific values within the parent chart's values.yaml file is impractical for large projects. Helm provides systematic mechanisms to propagate configuration parameters across these levels, primarily through the values.yaml files and the use of the .Values object in templates.

The recommended pattern for parameter passing involves names-pacing subchart values within the parent chart's values.yaml, un-der keys named after the subcharts. For example, consider a par-ent chart named webapp that includes a database subchart:

```
database:
  replicaCount: 3
  persistence:
    enabled: true
```

Within the database subchart, templates access these values via .Values.replicaCount and .Values.persistence.enabled. When rendered as part of the parent chart, Helm automatically merges the parent's database key values into the subchart scope, preserving encapsulation while allowing overrides.

To facilitate reusability, subcharts should provide sensible defaults within their own values.yaml files but remain fully configurable when embedded. It is considered best practice to avoid hard-coding configuration values inside templates, favoring parameteri-zation through values.yaml wherever possible to keep the deploy-ment flexible.

In dynamic environments, injecting values directly from environ-ment variables into Helm charts is crucial for aligning deployments with runtime contexts, such as different staging environments or cloud providers. Helm itself does not natively interpret environ-ment variables inside the values.yaml file, but this limitation can be overcome as follows.

One common method utilizes Helm's --set or --values flags during the helm install or helm upgrade commands along with shell substitution:

```
helm install webapp ./webapp \
  --set database.replicaCount=${DB_REPLICA_COUNT} \
  --set image.tag=${IMAGE_TAG}
```

This approach allows environment variables defined in the shell or CI/CD pipeline environment to directly parameterize Helm deployments without modifying chart files.

Alternatively, environment variables can be converted into a tailored YAML file prior to execution:

```
cat <<EOL > env-values.yaml
database:
  replicaCount: ${DB_REPLICA_COUNT}
image:
  tag: ${IMAGE_TAG}
EOL

helm install webapp ./webapp -f env-values.yaml
```

This intermediate step provides a repeatable and auditable values configuration aligned to the current environment and can be integrated seamlessly into automated pipelines.

Modern continuous integration and delivery systems afford robust parameterization through variable management and templating capabilities. Leveraging these pipeline features to externalize Helm chart configuration promotes automated, environment-specific deployments.

Within a CI/CD tool such as Jenkins, GitLab CI, or GitHub Actions, configuration parameters are managed as pipeline variables or secrets. These can be injected into Helm commands analogously to environment variables shown earlier. For example, a GitHub Actions workflow snippet performing a Helm upgrade might include:

```
- name: Deploy Helm Chart
  run: |
    helm upgrade --install webapp ./webapp \
      --set database.replicaCount=${{ secrets.DB_REPLICA_COUNT }}
      \
      --set image.tag=${{ env.IMAGE_TAG }}
  env:
    IMAGE_TAG: ${{ github.sha }}
```

Care must be taken to securely manage secrets and sensitive values using the pipeline's secure storage facilities. Additionally, parameter validation and defaulting within charts remain important since pipelines cannot guarantee completeness or correctness of input values.

Beyond environment variables, loading and managing configuration from external sources enhances modularity and centralizes operational control. Helm supports multiple ways to integrate such external data:

- Files from remote storage: Values files stored in artifact repositories, cloud storage buckets, or configuration management databases can be fetched during deployment. A common approach is scripting retrieval commands in the CI/CD pipeline before Helm execution, then referencing the downloaded file via the -f flag.

- Kubernetes ConfigMaps and Secrets: When running in Kubernetes, pre-existing ConfigMaps or Secrets can be referenced within Helm templates through resource objects or via Helm hooks. This enables separation of sensitive or environment-specific data from chart templates and values files.

- Parameter stores and vaults: External secret management systems like HashiCorp Vault, AWS Parameter Store, or Azure Key Vault are increasingly integrated with Helm via custom plugins or pre-deployment scripts. These inject parameters securely during the build or deploy phases, minimizing static credential exposure.

To optimize parameterization and external configuration:

- Design subcharts with clear, minimal required values; provide documented defaults.

- Namespace subchart values explicitly in parent values files to avoid collisions and clarify ownership.

- Limit logic in templates by relying on passed parameters rather than conditional code, fostering clarity.

- Automate value injection through CI/CD pipelines using environment variables, secrets, or external files to ensure traceability and separation of concerns.

- Employ validation mechanisms (e.g., Helm hooks, JSON schema validation in Helm 3) to verify parameter correctness pre-installation.

- Maintain declarative values rather than procedural generation where feasible, improving auditability.

- Secure secret values with encrypted stores and avoid committing them into version control.

Thoroughly applying these patterns establishes a scalable and maintainable Helm deployment infrastructure. It empowers teams to adapt deployments dynamically based on environment-specific or runtime contexts without compromising encapsulation or template integrity, thus enabling robust continuous delivery pipelines and operational consistency in cloud-native environments.

3.5. Chart Testing: Unit, Integration, and Smoke Tests

Implementing rigorous testing procedures is essential for maintaining the quality and reliability of Kubernetes Helm charts throughout their lifecycle. This section addresses methodologies to build quality assurance into charts, focusing on unit testing of templates, integration testing with test hooks, and deployment validation through smoke tests in sandbox environments. Together, these testing strategies form a comprehensive framework to detect issues early, verify chart correctness, and ensure stable deployments.

Unit testing isolates the individual template files within a Helm chart and verifies their rendered output against expected values. This allows developers to assert the correctness of template logic, conditional statements, templating functions, and variable substitutions without needing a live Kubernetes cluster.

The process typically involves invoking the Helm rendering engine (`helm template`) with controlled input values and capturing the resulting Kubernetes manifests. Testing tools such as `helm-unittest`, `unittest`, or `helm-test` enable defining assertions on the rendered YAML, for example, confirming the presence of specific fields, correct field values, or adherence to naming conventions.

A minimalist example using `helm-unittest` written as a YAML test file might look like:

```
suite: Deployment Template Test
templates:
  - deployment.yaml
tests:
  - it: should render the correct container image
    set:
      image.repository: nginx
      image.tag: 1.16
    asserts:
      - equal:
          path: spec.template.spec.containers[0].image
          value: nginx:1.16
  - it: should set replicas to 3 when specified
    set:
      replicaCount: 3
    asserts:
      - equal:
          path: spec.replicas
          value: 3
```

These tests run locally and provide immediate feedback on changes in template logic before packaging or deployment. Unit tests are invaluable for verifying the granular business logic embedded in Helm templates, such as conditional resource creation, label propagation, and Helm function behaviors.

Integration tests in the context of Helm charts validate the inter-action between the rendered resources and the target Kubernetes environment. Unlike unit tests, which focus on static template output, integration tests deploy charts to a controlled environment (e.g., a local Kubernetes cluster like Kind or Minikube) and verify runtime behaviors such as resource readiness, inter-service connectivity, and correct configuration.

One effective pattern to perform integration testing is to employ Helm test hooks, which run Kubernetes `Job` resources defined inside the chart after installation or upgrade. Annotated with `helm.sh/hook: test`, these jobs can execute commands testing deployed resources from within the cluster, thereby validating end-to-end functionality.

Example of a Helm test job hook manifest:

```
apiVersion: batch/v1
kind: Job
metadata:
  name: "{{ include "mychart.fullname" . }}-test-connection"
  annotations:
    "helm.sh/hook": test
spec:
  template:
    spec:
      containers:
      - name: test
        image: busybox
        command: ['sh', '-c', 'wget --spider --timeout=5 http://
    myservice:8080 || exit 1']
      restartPolicy: Never
```

Upon running `helm test <release>`, this job executes and attempts to reach the internal service endpoint, returning success only if connectivity is established. Such tests confirm that critical components are functional post-deployment.

Integration testing can be automated within Continuous Integration (CI) pipelines by sequentially installing the chart, waiting for pod readiness, running the Helm tests, and tearing down test clusters. Tools like `kind` or `minikube` ensure reproducible Kubernetes environments and simplify this process.

Smoke testing constitutes a lightweight verification step designed to quickly ascertain that a Helm chart deployment is fundamentally operational and does not introduce regressions in sandbox or staging environments. These tests are less granular than integration tests but more practical for frequent execution, serving as a gatekeeper before promoting deployments to production.

Smoke tests typically include:

- Verifying that all critical Kubernetes resources (Deployments, Services, ConfigMaps, Secrets) exist and are in the expected state.

- Confirming that pods enter the Ready state within a defined timeout.

- Checking key service endpoints for expected HTTP response codes or API readiness.

- Ensuring that no CrashLoopBackOff or persistent error state occurs within deployed workloads.

Automating smoke tests can be done using CLI commands combined with scripting tools or Kubernetes-native probes. A sample bash snippet performing basic smoke checks might be:

```
# Wait up to 120 seconds for all pods in the release namespace to
    be ready
kubectl wait --for=condition=Ready pod -l release=myrelease --
    timeout=120s

# Check service availability using curl inside temporary pod
kubectl run test-pod --rm -i --tty --image=curlimages/curl -- \
  curl -sf http://myservice.namespace.svc.cluster.local/healthz
```

A non-zero exit status or timeout indicates an unhealthy deployment that merits investigation.

Integrating smoke tests into CI/CD pipelines ensures that even rapid iterative changes undergo a sanity check before merging or promoting. When combined with unit and integration tests, smoke tests complete a tiered quality assurance strategy.

- **Unit testing** focuses on static template correctness without requiring cluster dependencies. It is essential for validating logic, templating functions, and configuration options rapidly during development.

- **Integration testing** exercises the actual deployed resources in a Kubernetes environment using Helm test hooks or external tools, confirming runtime interactions and readiness.

- **Smoke testing** performs quick validation of deployments in sandbox clusters, verifying deployment success and basic service health to catch regressions early.

Adopting these complementary testing strategies promotes robust Helm charts that behave as intended, improve maintainability, and increase confidence in automated deployments within Kubernetes environments.

A consistent practice is to automate and incorporate all three testing levels into the development and delivery pipelines to close feedback loops, reduce manual errors, and accelerate the release cadence without sacrificing reliability.

3.6. Linting, Validation, and Manifest Integrity

Releasing software to a container orchestration platform such as Kubernetes necessitates meticulous attention to the correctness and consistency of resource manifests. Ensuring manifest safety and reliability before deployment minimizes runtime errors, prevents rollout failures, and reduces downtime. This section examines robust mechanisms for catching errors early through static analysis, rigorous schema validation, and best practices for maintaining syntax integrity in Kubernetes manifests.

Static analysis of manifests, commonly referred to as linting, is an essential first line of defense. Tools designed for Kubernetes manifests analyze YAML or JSON resource descriptions without applying them to a cluster, identifying issues such as deprecated APIs, missing fields, incorrect data types, or policy violations. By systematically scrutinizing the manifest structure and content, linters help developers adhere to cluster API conventions and best practices. Established linters like `kubectl`'s built-in `--dry-run` mode, or third-party tools such as `kubeval`, `kube-linter`, and `kubescore` provide comprehensive static checks. These tools combine structural validation with domain-specific heuristics, for example, verifying that container images adhere to specified registries, or that resource requests and limits follow organizational policies.

Schema validation complements linting by enforcing strict adherence to the Kubernetes API resource schemas documented via OpenAPI specifications. While linting focuses on common issues and best practices, schema validation verifies the manifest against the formal typed definition of each resource kind and API version. This guarantees that required fields are present, enumerations conform to expected values, and data types match their declared formats. Schema validation is particularly vital in complex deployment pipelines where manifests might be composed or templated dynamically, potentially introducing subtle errors. Tools like `kubeval` and `conftest` harness Kubernetes OpenAPI schemas to provide this layer of rigorous verification. They can be integrated into CI/CD pipelines to reject manifests that fail schema conformance before they traverse further stages.

Maintaining syntax integrity is a foundational aspect underpinning both linting and schema validation. YAML manifests, due to their indentation sensitivity and relatively loose syntax compared to JSON, are susceptible to structural errors invisible to simple textual diff tools. Common syntax pitfalls include inconsistent indentation, missing document delimiters, or improper quoting of strings containing special characters. Such errors commonly manifest as cryptic parser errors upon applying manifests, leading to frustrating debugging sessions. Employing YAML parsers in validation stages or editors with YAML-aware plugins can detect and rectify these issues early. Additionally, converting YAML manifests into JSON and back can act as a normalization step, enforcing consistent formatting and uncovering hidden syntax flaws.

Integrating these verification steps into the release workflow mandates automation to scale and enforce standards uniformly. A typical pipeline stage would first perform linting to catch common policy violations and style issues. Upon passing linting, manifests undergo schema validation to ensure conformance to Kubernetes API definitions. Finally, some pipelines incorporate manifest signing or checksum verification to guarantee integrity and immutability of the manifests during promotion stages, precluding unauthorized modifications. Adopting a "fail fast" philosophy ensures that errors are detected as soon as possible, preventing faulty manifests from advancing to cluster application or promotion into production.

In practice, the following example illustrates a command sequence employing `kubeval` for validation within a pipeline:

```
kubeval --schema-location default ./manifests/deployment.yaml
```

This command validates the given manifest against the Kubernetes cluster's default OpenAPI schema, returning detailed diagnostic messages for any deviations.

The output in case of an invalid manifest might be:

```
The document deployment.yaml contains an invalid Deployment
-- deployment.spec.template.spec.containers[0].resources.requests.cpu: Invali
d type. Expected: string
```

Such explicit feedback enables rapid correction of resource definition issues such as erroneous data types.

Besides tooling, best practices contribute significantly to manifest integrity. These include:

- Consistent use of API versions aligned with the target Kubernetes cluster version. Periodic auditing for deprecated APIs reduces the risk of abrupt failures caused by upgraded clusters.

- Modularization of manifests using templating engines or kustomize overlays, which promote reuse and reduce duplication-related errors.

- Avoidance of inline environment variable expansions or unvalidated parameters that might introduce syntactical flaws.

- Incorporation of comments and descriptive field annotations to clarify intent, improving maintainability and easing future analysis.

- Version control of manifests with pull request reviews including automated linting and validation checks.

By combining automated linting, comprehensive schema validation, stringent syntax verification, and disciplined manifest management, teams significantly mitigate the risk of propagating errors into production clusters. The resulting increases in deployment reliability and operational stability are invaluable for large-scale or security-critical applications, where resiliency and correctness are paramount. Ensuring manifest integrity thus becomes an indispensable practice for any mature Kubernetes workflow.

Chapter 4

Managing Secrets and Sensitive Data with Helm

In the intricate realm of Kubernetes, secrets are both a necessity and a notorious source of risk. This chapter dives deep into the strategies for managing secrets and sensitive data using Helm—balancing usability, automation, and security at every turn. Discover the patterns and integrations that make secure deployments scalable, audit-friendly, and future-proof against evolving compliance requirements.

4.1. Kubernetes Secrets: Native Support and Limitations

Kubernetes provides a native mechanism for managing sensitive information through its `Secret` resource type, designed to handle data such as passwords, OAuth tokens, SSH keys, and other confidential information required by applications. The primary objective is to furnish a seamless and standardized method for injecting secrets into containerized workloads without embedding them directly within application images or configuration manifests.

By default, Kubernetes stores secrets as base64-encoded strings within etcd, the distributed key-value store underpinning the cluster state. This design choice implies that secret data is persisted alongside other cluster information, relying on the security of etcd for confidentiality. The base64 encoding is not encryption but simply an encoding format, which leaves secret data exposed unless further protection is applied. Kubernetes supports encryption of secrets at rest through integration with etcd's built-in encryption providers. When enabled, Kubernetes encrypts secret data before writing it to etcd to protect it from unauthorized access in the storage backend.

Enabling encryption at rest requires configuring the EncryptionConfiguration resource referenced in the Kubernetes API server manifest. The encryption providers available include aescbc, secretbox, kms (integration with external Key Management Services), and identity (no encryption). The aescbc provider is commonly used for symmetric encryption with AES in CBC mode but demands proper key management to ensure security. Critical considerations include secure key rotation practices and ensuring strict API server access controls.

Access to secrets within the Kubernetes ecosystem is primarily controlled via Kubernetes Role-Based Access Control (RBAC). By default, secrets are accessible to pods through environment variables or mounted volumes if the pod specification explicitly requests them, and subject to namespace scoping. The default permissions restrict secret access to users and service accounts with granted roles. Nevertheless, these access controls are coarse-grained and susceptible to misconfiguration, potentially allowing privilege escalation or unnecessary exposure of secrets to components that do not require them.

While Kubernetes secrets streamline management of sensitive data by preventing embedding secrets in container images or configuration files, several inherent limitations constrain their effectiveness as a comprehensive secrets management solution.

- The default storage mechanism in etcd is vulnerable if the encryption-at-rest feature is not enabled or improperly configured. In such cases, anyone with read access to etcd can retrieve plaintext secrets. Moreover, etcd backups may inadvertently capture secrets, necessitating careful handling and encryption of backup data.

- Kubernetes secrets do not provide built-in lifecycle management capabilities such as automatic secret rotation, expiry, or revocation. Secrets are immutable objects within the cluster until explicitly updated or deleted, requiring external processes or operators to enforce rotation policies. This limitation increases the administrative burden and risk of stale or compromised secrets persisting in the system.

- The method of injecting secrets as environment variables or mounted volumes carries exposure risks. Environment variables may be logged or exposed in process listings or debug traces, while mounted secrets as files persist in container file systems and may be accessible beyond intended boundaries. Additionally, secrets mounted as files by default are stored in tmpfs or memory-backed filesystems, which mitigates disk persistence but does not address in-memory attack vectors.

- Kubernetes lacks built-in integration for advanced secret management functionalities such as dynamic secret generation, leasing, or fine-grained audit trails. As demand for enterprise-grade security grows, teams often rely on third-party secret management tools (e.g., HashiCorp Vault, AWS

Secrets Manager, or Azure Key Vault) to complement Kubernetes secrets. These external systems provide features including credential generation on demand, automated secret renewal, strong audit logging, and robust access controls, often integrated via Kubernetes Custom Resource Definitions (CRDs) or CSI volume drivers.

Kubernetes supports secrets natively with mechanisms for storage, basic encryption, and access control, providing foundational confidentiality benefits for containerized environments. However, the default implementations have notable constraints in storage security, lifecycle management, and operational exposure that necessitate supplementary approaches. To achieve robust secrets management aligned with stringent security requirements, organizations must layer additional tooling, policies, and infrastructure integrations on top of Kubernetes' native secret capabilities.

4.2. Helm's Approach to Secret Management

Helm, as a Kubernetes package manager, provides a powerful framework for defining, installing, and upgrading complex Kubernetes applications through charts. Integral to these applications is the management of sensitive information-credentials, tokens, keys, and other secrets-that require careful handling throughout their lifecycle. This section delves into Helm's role in secret management, encompassing integration strategies for secret data within chart values, appropriate workflows to safeguard this sensitive information, common anti-patterns to avoid, and recommended practices for templating with secrets securely.

Integration of Secrets into Helm Charts

Helm charts conventionally accept configuration via the `values.yaml` file or explicitly supplied value overrides. Embedding secrets directly into `values.yaml` is generally discouraged due to risks associated with version control exposure and plaintext persistence. Instead, secrets should be incorporated through externalized means, either by referencing pre-existing Kubernetes Secret resources or by injecting sensitive data at deployment time through Helm's value overrides.

The common patterns for secret integration are:

- *Referencing Kubernetes Secrets*: Charts specify Kubernetes Secret objects as part of the manifest templates, typically using `{{ .Values.secretName }}` to indicate the secret to mount or access.

- *Supplying Secrets via Helm Value Overrides*: Sensitive data can be passed at installation or upgrade time using the `--set` flag or separate value files provided with `--values`, ensuring secrets are not stored within version control.

- *Use of External Secret Management Systems*: Systems like HashiCorp Vault, External Secrets Operator, or Sealed Secrets can be integrated with Helm workflows, where secrets are dynamically fetched or decrypted upon deployment.

By externalizing secrets, Helm charts remain declarative and portable without hardcoding sensitive values, aligning with best practices for secure software supply chains.

Workflows for Handling Sensitive Data in Helm Deployments

The secret management lifecycle involves secret creation, storage, transmission, consumption, and eventual rotation or revocation. Helm facilitates secret handling primarily in the deployment phase but must be orchestrated alongside secure upstream and downstream processes.

A robust workflow typically follows these steps:

83

1. *Secret Creation and Storage*: Secrets are generated and securely stored using Kubernetes Secrets or external vault technologies. Creation is automated or managed manually but must be tracked outside Helm's chart definitions.

2. *Secret Injection into Helm Releases*: When performing `helm install` or `helm upgrade`, secrets are injected either by referencing existing Secrets or by supplying secret values via secure means (e.g., environment variables, encrypted files).

3. *Secure Templating*: Templating logic within Helm charts incorporates secrets where required, for example, mounting Secrets as volumes or injecting values into container environment variables.

4. *Execution and Audit*: Helm executes Kubernetes API calls to create or update Secrets as per the chart templates. Audit trails must be maintained in the cluster and deployment automation to detect unauthorized access.

5. *Secret Rotation and Updates*: Periodic secret rotation requires seamless updating of Secret resources and rebooting or redeploying pods to consume new values. Helm `upgrade` can facilitate this but must coordinate with external rotation policies.

Automation tools such as CI/CD pipelines often provide the critical linkage, ensuring secrets are injected at deployment time without human exposure.

Anti-Patterns in Helm Secret Management

Despite Helm's flexibility, several anti-patterns compromise secret security or operational reliability:

- *Hardcoding Secrets in `values.yaml`*: Embedding plaintext secrets in default or committed values files leads to exposure risks within Git repositories or Helm chart artifacts.

84

- *Using Helm to Directly Manage Secret Values*: Helm templating to create Secrets with literal sensitive data can result in secrets being stored in the Helm release history and ConfigMaps, susceptible to cluster role-based access control (RBAC) overreach.

- *Storing Secrets in Helm Release Metadata*: Helm's release storage encodes all deployed manifests, including secrets, often in base64 encoded form in ConfigMaps or Secrets under the `kube-system` namespace, potentially increasing the attack surface.

- *Passing Sensitive Data on Command Lines*: Using `--set` or environment variables on CLI commands can leave traces in shell histories or process tables.

Avoidance of these patterns is essential to reduce the risk of secret leakage and aligns with the principle of least privilege and separation of concerns.

Safe Templating Practices for Secrets

Helm's Go templating engine affords powerful processing but demands caution when handling secrets. Safe templating techniques include:

- *Referencing Existing Kubernetes Secrets Rather Than Declaring Secrets Inline*: Templates should assume secret existence rather than generate new secret manifests with embedded sensitive values.

- *Minimal Exposure in Logs and Outputs*: Conditional guards and careful use of `printf` or `quote` functions prevent accidental logging of secrets during template rendering.

- *Templating Security Contexts and Volume Mounts Without Secret Disclosure*: Templates should use placeholders from

.Values or external references to ensure secrets are only referenced via Kubernetes mechanisms like volume mounts or environment variables from Secrets.

- *Avoid Using Helm Functions That Reveal or Duplicate Secret Data*: Functions that stringify or manipulate secrets should be used sparingly, ensuring no indirect disclosure occurs.

A typical safe templating snippet for environment variables looks as follows:

```
env:
- name: DB_PASSWORD
  valueFrom:
    secretKeyRef:
      name: {{ .Values.db.secretName }}
      key: password
```

This approach ensures credentials remain within Kubernetes Secret objects and are not embedded in plain text within Helm manifests, reducing exposure within Helm release metadata.

Helm's approach to secret management emphasizes declarative, externalized secrets, secure injection at deployment time, and careful templating that avoids secret leakage. It integrates effectively within broader secret management lifecycles when combined with robust external tooling and operational discipline. Avoiding antipatterns and adopting safe templating practices are indispensable to maintain the confidentiality and integrity of sensitive data in Kubernetes environments orchestrated by Helm.

4.3. Using Helm with External Secret Managers

Helm, as a Kubernetes package manager, simplifies the deployment of applications and services through templated manifests. However, managing sensitive information within

86

Helm charts presents a significant challenge, given the inherent risk of embedding secrets directly in plaintext manifest files or values. Integrating Helm with external secret management solutions enhances security by allowing centralized secret storage, automated retrieval, and robust access controls. This section focuses on practical approaches to connect Helm deployments with popular external secret managers: HashiCorp Vault, AWS Secrets Manager, and Mozilla SOPS, detailing mechanisms that facilitate secure and automated secret handling within Kubernetes environments.

Integrating Helm with HashiCorp Vault

HashiCorp Vault is a widely adopted secrets management system that provides a secure API for storing and retrieving sensitive data. Integrating Vault with Helm involves a few different architectural patterns, including pre-render secret injection, Vault sidecar agents, and Helm plugins that fetch secrets dynamically.

One typical approach leverages the Vault Agent Injector which enables automatic injection of secrets into Pods as files or environment variables without storing them in Kubernetes manifests or Helm values. Helm charts are configured to deploy sidecar containers running Vault Agents alongside application containers. The application manifests specify annotations instructing the Vault Injector on what secrets to mount.

Alternatively, Helm's template rendering phase can integrate with Vault by invoking Vault CLI or API calls to fetch secrets prior to template installation. This is often done using custom Helm plugins or scripts that retrieve Vault secrets and populate Helm's values.yaml dynamically.

For example, a simple Vault CLI fetch can be scripted before invoking Helm:

```
export DB_PASSWORD=$(vault kv get -field=password secret/data/db)
helm install myapp ./chart --set db.password=$DB_PASSWORD
```

This workflow ensures secrets are never persisted as plaintext in Helm charts or container images.

More sophisticated usage involves leveraging HashiCorp's Helm Secrets plugin, which enables encrypting `values.yaml` files with Vault-managed keys, decrypting them at install or upgrade time:

```
helm secrets enc values.yaml
helm secrets upgrade --install myapp ./chart -f values.yaml.dec
```

The plugin uses Vault's transit secrets engine for encryption and decryption, maintaining end-to-end secrecy even in version control systems.

Leveraging AWS Secrets Manager with Helm

AWS Secrets Manager offers a scalable secret lifecycle and access management service tightly integrated with IAM and AWS ecosystems. To incorporate AWS Secrets Manager in Helm-based workflows, the most common patterns involve:

- Pre-fetching secrets with automation scripts: Similar to Vault, automation scripts or CI/CD pipelines invoke AWS CLI or SDKs to retrieve secrets at deployment time, then provide them as Helm values overrides.

```
export API_KEY=$(aws secretsmanager get-secret-value --secret-id
    myapi | jq -r '.SecretString')
helm upgrade --install app ./chart --set api.key=$API_KEY
```

- Using Kubernetes External Secrets (KES) or External Secrets Operator: These tools reconcile Kubernetes `Secret` resources from AWS Secrets Manager dynamically. Helm charts benefit by referencing the Kubernetes secrets generated by KES, sidestepping the need to embed sensitive data directly:

```
apiVersion: external-secrets.io/v1beta1
kind: ExternalSecret
```

88

```
metadata:
  name: app-secret
spec:
  refreshInterval: 1h
  secretStoreRef:
    name: aws-secret-store
    kind: SecretStore
  target:
    name: app-k8s-secret
  data:
  - secretKey: api-key
    remoteRef:
      key: myapi
      property: apiKey
```

Helm templates can then consume this Kubernetes secret nor-mally:

```
env:
- name: API_KEY
  valueFrom:
    secretKeyRef:
      name: app-k8s-secret
      key: api-key
```

This decouples secret management from Helm releases, providing rotation and auditing via AWS Secrets Manager independently.

Employing Mozilla SOPS for Secret Encryption within Helm Charts

Mozilla SOPS (Secrets OPerationS) is an encryption utility designed for encrypting structured files such as YAML or JSON. It integrates with Helm by encrypting sensitive sections of values.yaml or entire Kubernetes manifest files and decrypting them automatically during deployments.

SOPS supports multiple Key Management Systems (KMS), includ-ing AWS KMS, GCP KMS, Azure Key Vault, and PGP keys, enabling portability and vendor neutrality. Encrypted values files can be safely stored in version control systems, mitigating secret leakage risks.

A typical workflow involves encrypting the secret values file using

SOPS:

```
sops -e -i values.yaml
```

During deployment, a Helm plugin or helper command decrypts the file before invoking Helm:

```
sops -d values.yaml | helm upgrade --install myapp ./chart -f -
```

Alternatively, Helm Secrets, mentioned previously for Vault, is compatible with SOPS out-of-the-box, providing a unified CLI for managing encrypted charts regardless of the underlying KMS.

SOPS-encrypted manifests enable secure storage of Kubernetes secrets alongside application configurations without exposing plaintext, while retaining compatibility with standard Helm workflows.

Comparative Considerations and Best Practices

When selecting and integrating an external secret manager with Helm, several factors influence design decisions:

- Security model and audit capability: Vault offers granular policies and detailed audit trails, suited for complex enterprise environments, whereas cloud-native solutions like AWS Secrets Manager leverage cloud-native identity and access management.

- Secret lifecycle automation: External Secrets Operators provide Kubernetes-native reconciliation, ideal for continuous secret synchronization independent of Helm lifecycle, reducing the risk of stale secrets.

- Operational complexity and tooling: Some approaches require additional components like sidecar containers or custom Helm plugins, increasing maintenance overhead.

- Version control and code review workflows: SOPS or Helm Secrets facilitate safe storage of encrypted secrets in Git repositories, preserving GitOps compatibility.

A common advanced deployment architecture combines these tools: using Vault or AWS Secrets Manager for centralized secret storage and rotation, Kubernetes External Secrets or Vault Injectors to project secrets into cluster-native `Secret` volumes, and SOPS/Helm Secrets for managing encrypted Helm overrides in Git-driven pipelines.

Secret Manager	Integration Method	Typical Use Case
HashiCorp Vault	Vault Agent sidecars; Helm Secrets plugin; Pre-render scripts	High-security enterprise with complex access control
AWS Secrets Manager	CLI pre-fetch; Kubernetes External Secrets	AWS-centric workflows with native IAM and automatic sync
Mozilla SOPS	Encrypt values.yaml; Helm Secrets plugin for decryption	GitOps workflows requiring encrypted manifests in VCS

In all cases, secrets should never be stored as plaintext within Helm chart repositories or container images. Instead, these external secret management strategies enforce segregation of duties, minimize exposure risk, and facilitate automated, secure secret distribution throughout Kubernetes clusters while preserving Helm's declarative deployment advantages.

4.4. Injecting and Rotating Secrets in Multi-Environment Deployments

Secure management of secrets such as API keys, database credentials, and cryptographic material in multi-environment deployments requires systematic approaches that ensure confidentiality, integrity, and availability throughout the deployment lifecycle. Injection and rotation of secrets must be designed to minimize human interaction, adhere to the principle of least privilege, and support automation at scale.

Secret Injection at Deploy Time

Injecting secrets securely at deployment time demands a mechanism that avoids embedding sensitive data in source code, container images, or configuration files stored in version control. Instead, secrets should be dynamically retrieved and provisioned by the deployment pipeline or runtime environment through controlled access.

A widely adopted pattern is to utilize dedicated secrets management systems such as HashiCorp Vault, AWS Secrets Manager, or Azure Key Vault. These systems provide APIs enabling ephemeral retrieval of secrets with access governed by fine-grained identity and access management (IAM) policies. Deployment tools such as Kubernetes operators, CI/CD runners, or infrastructure automation frameworks can request secrets just before or during application initialization.

For example, in a Kubernetes environment, secrets can be injected via environment variables or volume mounts sourced from secrets stored in the cluster or retrieved on-demand by sidecar containers. When leveraging sidecars, a small agent can authenticate with the secret store, dynamically fetch secrets, and cache them locally, decoupling secret access from the main application container and reducing risk in case of compromise.

The injection workflow should enforce zero secret exposure in pipeline logs by sanitizing outputs and using secured logging options. Pipeline credentials accessing secret stores must themselves follow least privilege, for example by authorizing only the specific pipeline job or environment namespace to retrieve needed secrets.

Least Privilege and Access Controls

To enforce least privilege, secrets management must depend on strong identity verification tied to the deployment environment context. Techniques include:

- **Short-lived tokens:** Use limited lifetime tokens for authentication to secret stores, automatically refreshed and revoked.

- **Environment-scoped policies:** Define access scopes per deployment stage (development, staging, production) with non-overlapping permissions.

- **Role-based access control (RBAC):** Assign minimum roles to pipelines and runtime workloads, minimizing cross-environment leakage.

For instance, production environments should never share service accounts or tokens with non-production environments. Externalizing role assignment and authorization audits ensures modifications are tracked and can be automatically verified.

Automated Credential Rotation

Regular rotation of credentials is vital to limit exposure risk in case of secret compromise. Manual rotation is error-prone and can cause application downtime; thus automation is essential.

An exemplary rotation pattern consists of the following steps coordinated between the secret store and the consuming application:

- Generate new secret version in secret store.

- Update access permissions for new secret version.

- Notify application or trigger redeploy to reload secret.

- Application seamlessly transitions to new secret version.

- Revoke and delete old secret version after grace period.

Applications should be designed to support rolling reloads or hot-swapping of secrets without restart, using mechanisms such as signal handlers or dedicated configuration reload endpoints. This enables zero-downtime rotation.

Using versioned secrets in the store further enhances safety, allowing rollback if the new secret is invalid or leads to failures.

Minimizing Human Error through Automation

Minimizing manual intervention reduces the risk of accidental exposure or misconfiguration. Confidence in automated secret injection and rotation pipelines depends on comprehensive integration with CI/CD systems, configuration management, and observability tooling.

Key practices include:

- **Infrastructure as Code (IaC):** Define all secret-related configuration, policies, and roles declaratively and versioned in source control.

- **Pipeline validation:** Integrate automated tests to verify secret injection steps and access controls before production rollout.

- **Audit logging and alerting:** Maintain immutable logs of secret access and rotation events, with real-time alerts on unusual activity or failures.

- **Secret scanning:** Employ automated scanning tools to detect potential secret leakage in artifacts and code bases.

Automated workflows can leverage templating and parameterization to reduce configuration drift across environments, ensuring consistent secret handling. Cross-environment orchestration tools help synchronize secret versions and validate environment-specific parameters to prevent credential misuse.

Integration Patterns Across Multiple Environments

In multi-environment deployments, secrets often differ between stages due to environment-specific endpoints, keys, or regulatory contexts. Strategies to accommodate this include:

- **Hierarchical secret namespaces:** Organize secrets in the store under structured paths

94

representing environment and application segments, e.g., prod/database/credentials vs.
dev/database/credentials.

- **Environment metadata tagging:** Attach environment labels to secrets and access policies to enforce correct contextual usage.

- **Environment-specific roles and identities:** Assign
  unique service identities per environment to isolate secret
  retrieval scope.

These patterns reduce the chance of cross-environment contami-
nation and allow precise control over secret lifecycle per environment.

Example: Injecting and Rotating Secrets in Kubernetes

Consider a microservice deployed across dev, staging, and prod
namespaces in Kubernetes, utilizing HashiCorp Vault to manage
secrets.

```
# Vault policy for prod environment access
path "secret/data/prod/*" {
  capabilities = ["read", "list"]
}
```

The deployment pipeline authenticates with Vault via Kubernetes
service account tokens, restricted to namespace-specific Vault policies. At deploy time, a Vault agent sidecar fetches secrets from
secret/data/prod/service and mounts them as files into the application pod.

Rotation is scheduled via a Vault renewal job which creates new
secrets, updates policies, and triggers Kubernetes rolling updates
through the deployment controller:

```
kubectl rollout restart deployment/my-service -n prod
```

This controlled, automated cycle minimizes downtime, enforces least privilege, and reduces operational complexity.

These integrated patterns provide a robust foundation for securely injecting and rotating secrets across complex, multi-environment deployments. Employing automation and fine-grained access control is paramount to managing risks and operational efficiencies in modern software delivery pipelines.

4.5. Sealed Secrets and GitOps Secure Workflows

GitOps has transformed the approach toward application deployment and infrastructure management by treating Git repositories as the single source of truth for both. However, this model introduces significant challenges when dealing with sensitive data such as API keys, certificates, and encryption keys. Addressing these challenges demands mechanisms that preserve the core GitOps principles-declarative configuration, version control, and automated deployments-while safeguarding secrets in a manner compliant with stringent regulatory frameworks. Sealed Secrets and encrypted manifests emerge as pivotal technologies enabling secure GitOps workflows with full auditability and traceability.

At the heart of secure GitOps is the conundrum of secret management: how to store, version, and deploy secrets without exposing them in plaintext or risking accidental leakage. Traditional Git repositories are inherently public or internally shared and not designed for sensitive data storage. Storing secrets in plaintext conflicts with security best practices and regulatory mandates, such as HIPAA, PCI-DSS, or GDPR, which require strong controls over sensitive information and comprehensive auditing capabilities.

Sealed Secrets, introduced by Bitnami, represents a Kubernetes-native solution that encrypts secrets into a format safe for public repositories while enabling automated decryption and deployment. The core concept involves a public-private key cryptosystem where the private key resides deterministically within the Kubernetes cluster, and the public key is used to encrypt secrets before committing them to Git. This asymmetric encryption guarantees that only the targeted Kubernetes cluster can decrypt and use the secret, providing strong separation between stored and operational data.

The workflow begins with the `kubeseal` CLI tool, which runs locally and encrypts a standard Kubernetes `Secret` manifest into a SealedSecret. This SealedSecret is a custom Kubernetes resource, safe to store in version control systems:

```
kubectl create secret generic db-credentials \
  --from-literal=username=admin \
  --from-literal=password='s3cr3t!' \
  --dry-run=client -o yaml > secret.yaml

kubeseal --format=yaml < secret.yaml > sealedsecret.yaml
```

The resulting `sealedsecret.yaml` contains ciphertext immutable to unauthorized modifications, without preventing repository-level versioning and auditing. Version control retains all changes to the secret manifest, ensuring traceability of when and how secrets evolve, which is essential for compliance audits and incident investigation.

Deployment automation leverages Kubernetes controllers that monitor the Git repository for changes in SealedSecrets. Upon detection, the Sealed Secrets Controller running inside the cluster decrypts the manifest with its private key, creating standard Kubernetes `Secret` objects consumed by applications. The controller rejects invalid or corrupted manifests, assuring integrity and preventing potential rollback of secrets to previous versions without explicit commit history review.

Enhancing compliance, the encrypted manifest approach integrates seamlessly with GitOps pipelines, preserving the immutability and audit trails characteristic of source control systems. Every commit that alters a SealedSecret or encrypted manifest corresponds directly to a discrete change in secrets, including author, timestamp, and commit message. This chain of custody enables organizations to satisfy regulatory requirements requiring detailed records of who accessed or changed sensitive data and when.

Encrypted manifests generalize the concept beyond Sealed Secrets by enabling encryption of any Kubernetes manifest containing sensitive fields. Tools such as Mozilla SOPS or Mozilla's age can encrypt entire YAML files or fragments, supporting various key management systems, including GCP KMS, AWS KMS, Azure Key Vault, or PGP keys. This flexibility allows organizations to align encryption mechanisms with existing infrastructure and compliance mandates.

Consider the following example using *SOPS* to encrypt a manifest describing database credentials:

```
sops --encrypt --output=secret.enc.yaml secret.yaml
git add secret.enc.yaml
git commit -m "Add encrypted database credentials"
git push origin main
```

Within the GitOps pipeline, an automated decryption step configured with proper permissions retrieves the plaintext at deployment time and applies it securely to the cluster, ensuring no plaintext secrets persist in Git. Traceability is maintained by the commit history at the file level and the audit logs of the key management system authorizing decryption.

Critical to regulated environments is defining strict access controls on decryption keys, minimizing the risk of unauthorized disclosure. Key rotation policies, audit logging of key use, and integration with Identity and Access Management (IAM) frameworks enforce such controls. Sealed Secrets simplify key management by anchoring the private key inside the cluster, reducing the attack surface of external key storage.

The combination of Sealed Secrets and encrypted manifests enables security-conscious GitOps workflows that:

- **Maintain Confidentiality:** Secrets remain encrypted and unreadable within the Git repository, preventing snapshot leaks by insiders or attackers.

- **Ensure Integrity:** Encryption coupled with digital signatures or cryptographic verification prevents tampering or unauthorized rollback of secret manifests.

- **Preserve Auditability:** Every change to secret manifests is version-controlled, with metadata that supports audit trails required in governance frameworks.

- **Support Automation at Scale:** Decryption and application of secrets are automated within the cluster, enabling continuous delivery without manual secret injection.

- **Enable Compliance:** Align secret management with industry-specific regulations through encryption standards, key management policies, and access controls documented by version tracking.

Integrating Sealed Secrets into GitOps pipelines also facilitates multi-environment secret management, where multiple clusters possess unique private keys. The same encrypted manifest can be deployed safely in different clusters without exposing secrets, ensuring separation of concerns and environment-specific security policies.

Leveraging Sealed Secrets and encrypted manifests for GitOps workflows presents a robust strategy to fulfill the dual mandates of automation and security. By embedding encryption at the manifest layer, organizations gain a powerful mechanism to secure sensitive configuration while safeguarding the traceability and auditability critical for compliance-driven cloud-native operations.

This approach enables GitOps to extend beyond code and infrastructure, encompassing secure secret management as a foundational pillar of modern DevSecOps practices.

4.6. Auditing and Compliance for Secret Distribution

The security of secret distribution systems depends not only on robust access controls and encryption mechanisms but also on the ability to create comprehensive audit trails and enforce compliance policies effectively. Maintaining reliable and tamper-evident logs, tracking secret usage, and implementing lifecycle management are critical to both operational security and regulatory adherence. This section analyzes key techniques and best practices that ensure transparency, accountability, and incident readiness in secret distribution architectures.

Comprehensive Audit Trail Construction

Audit trails serve as the backbone of security accountability, enabling organizations to reconstruct events leading to data disclosures or policy violations. A robust audit system must capture a detailed record of all secret-related activities including creation, access, modification, deletion, and distribution events. The recording of these events should feature immutable timestamps, cryptographic integrity guarantees, and comprehensive metadata encompassing the identity of requesting entities, target secrets, access context, and results of authorization checks.

The adoption of append-only log structures, such as Merkle trees or blockchain-based ledgers, provides strong tamper-resistance. For instance, leveraging a Merkle tree hash-chain permits efficient verification of log integrity without full log transparency. This is particularly valuable in distributed secret management systems where decentralized or federated trust models are employed.

Technically, daily log generation can be encapsulated as follows within a typical secret management service:

```
class MerkleLog:
    def __init__(self):
        self.leaves = []
        self.root = None

    def append_event(self, event_data):
        event_hash = hash_function(event_data)
        self.leaves.append(event_hash)
        self.root = self.compute_merkle_root()

    def compute_merkle_root(self):
        current_level = self.leaves[:]
        while len(current_level) > 1:
            # Pairwise hash concatenation
            next_level = []
            for i in range(0, len(current_level), 2):
                left = current_level[i]
                right = current_level[i+1] if i+1 < len(
    current_level) else left
                combined = hash_function(left + right)
                next_level.append(combined)
            current_level = next_level
        return current_level[0] if current_level else None

def hash_function(data):
    import hashlib
    return hashlib.sha256(data.encode('utf-8')).hexdigest()
```

This cryptographic proof of log integrity supports auditing actions and compliance audits without exposing secret content or sensitive metadata unnecessarily.

Tracking Secret Usage and Access Patterns

Continuous monitoring of access patterns is essential for detecting unauthorized or anomalous use of secrets. Effective tracking solutions incorporate real-time logging of access events, with contextual attributes such as geographic location, device fingerprints, operation type, and user roles. Integrations with Identity and Access Management (IAM) systems enrich access logs with user identity verification status and multi-factor authentication events, thereby increasing granularity and forensic value.

Special attention is required to correlate secret usage with system or application behavior. This can be realized by embedding usage tokens or trace identifiers within API calls that retrieve secrets, enabling downstream tracing from secret request to final consumption. Such end-to-end traceability facilitates rapid diagnosis during incident investigations.

Periodic automated analysis of usage logs employing anomaly detection algorithms or rule-based engines can flag deviations from expected usage patterns. For example, bursts of secret access from unusual IP addresses or an uncharacteristic number of retrieval attempts in a short time frame signal potential compromise or insider threats.

Enforcing Compliance Through Policy-Driven Secret Lifecycle Management

Compliance frameworks such as GDPR, HIPAA, or PCI-DSS often mandate rigorous controls on secret handling, retention periods, and auditability. To satisfy these requirements, secret management systems should embed policy engines capable of enforcing lifecycle constraints automatically.

Lifecycle management procedures encompass:

- **Provisioning and Classification:** Secrets must be assigned sensitivity labels and expiration timestamps at creation. Classification dictates access levels and handling rules.

- **Rotation and Revocation:** Scheduled rotation policies ensure secrets are periodically replaced or disabled, thus reducing risk of compromise from prolonged exposure.

- **Archival and Secure Deletion:** At end-of-life, secrets should be securely archived with access restrictions or irreversibly deleted following cryptographic erasure standards.

- **Access Approval Workflows:** Multi-layered approval

processes for secret retrieval implement separation of duties and minimize unauthorized usage.

These lifecycle states and transitions must be explicitly logged and verifiable to demonstrate adherence to compliance mandates, forming an audit-ready record trail.

Incident Response Readiness and Forensic Capabilities

An effective incident response strategy for secret distribution anomalies presupposes timely detection and a comprehensive forensic dataset. Audit logs must be normalized and centralized in Security Information and Event Management (SIEM) systems capable of correlating secret access logs with broader network and endpoint telemetry. This cross-correlation enhances contextual understanding and accelerates root cause analysis.

To preserve evidentiary integrity, logs and forensic artifacts must be stored with cryptographic signing and protected against tampering and unauthorized deletion. Role-based access to forensic data is critical, as is maintaining clear chain-of-custody documentation.

Beyond reactive response, audit data supports proactive threat hunting and vulnerability assessments. Extraction of patterns and trends from historical logs can guide policy refinement, anomaly detection rule tuning, and privilege minimization efforts.

Summary of Best Practices

Key principles for auditing and compliance in secret distribution include:

- Implement immutable and cryptographically verifiable audit trails that cover all secret lifecycle events.

- Collect detailed access metadata to support granular usage monitoring and anomaly detection.

- Automate compliance enforcement through integrated life-

cycle management policies aligned with regulatory requirements.

- Centralize and secure logs for incident response prepared-
ness, ensuring forensic integrity and access controls.

- Employ continuous analysis and correlation of audit data to
reinforce defenses and support ongoing compliance.

The fusion of these techniques provides organizations with the
means to maintain robust security postures, satisfy stringent compliance audits, and minimize risks inherent in the distribution and
management of sensitive secrets.

Chapter 5

The Helm Release Lifecycle: Install, Upgrade, and Rollback

Shipping software with confidence in Kubernetes means orchestrating not just smooth installations, but robust upgrades and effortless rollbacks. This chapter peels back the layers of Helm's release lifecycle mechanisms, equipping you to manage change, track resources, and handle the unforeseen with precision. Get ready to master the art of reliable application delivery—where every release, from the first install to the latest upgrade, is both repeatable and recoverable.

5.1. Understanding Helm Releases and State Management

Helm, as a package manager for Kubernetes, encapsulates complex application deployments through abstractions that facilitate version control, configuration management, and lifecycle operations. Central to Helm's architecture is the concept of a *release*, which serves as an instantiation of a chart rendered with a particular set of configuration values and deployed into a Kubernetes cluster. Understanding how Helm models releases as versioned records and manages their state within the cluster is critical to leveraging Helm effectively in production-grade environments.

A **release** in Helm represents a single deployment of a chart with a specified name and namespace. Each release maintains a chronological history through discrete versions, enabling upgrade, rollback, and audit capabilities. When a chart is installed or upgraded, Helm generates a new release version, incrementing an internal sequence number. This versioning abstracts the underlying Kubernetes resource manifests, capturing the precise state transformations across the lifecycle of the application.

Helm tracks release state primarily through two mechanisms: local storage within the Helm client and persistent storage within the Kubernetes cluster. The latter is more authoritative and forms the basis for Helm's reconciliation logic. Upon installation, Helm stores release metadata and the rendered Kubernetes manifests as Kubernetes `Secrets` (or `ConfigMaps` depending on configuration) in the target namespace. Each release corresponds to a unique Secret manifest with labels that Helm uses for indexing and retrieval. This embedded metadata includes the `Chart` version, the applied values, the manifest content, timestamps, and the release status.

The storage of release information as Secrets has multiple implications:

- **Persistence and recovery**: Release details survive Helm client restarts or local state loss, enabling Helm to recover and manage releases accurately.

- **Concurrency and multi-client support**: Since release state is cluster-resident, multiple Helm clients or automation tools can operate on releases without relying on stale local caches.

- **Security considerations**: Since these Secrets include full manifests and values, sensitive information could be exposed if Secrets are not encrypted or restricted properly.

The recorded manifests in release Secrets correspond precisely to the output of the Helm rendering engine, where templates from the chart are combined with supplied configuration values to yield the Kubernetes resource definitions to be applied. This renders Helm effective as a declarative system that can replay previous release states to perform upgrades, rollbacks, or deletions.

The relationship between **charts**, **values**, and the resulting **Kubernetes resources** is foundational to understanding Helm's model:

- *Charts* are package artifacts representing an application or component, composed of a collection of Kubernetes manifests templated with the Go templating language. Charts provide a structure for resources (Deployments, Services, ConfigMaps, etc.) as parameterized manifests.

- *Values* are hierarchical data structures provided at install or upgrade time, specifying configuration parameters. These override default values declared in the chart. Values influence the rendered manifests by replacing template placeholders, enabling flexible customization without modifying the original chart.

- *Kubernetes resources* are the concrete manifests generated by template rendering. These definitions define the desired state that Kubernetes will strive to realize.

When a release is deployed, Helm executes the following core process:

- **Template rendering**: The chart's templates are rendered using the merged values (default plus overrides), producing a fully expanded set of Kubernetes manifests.

- **Resource application**: The rendered manifests are applied atomically to the cluster, typically through server-side apply or direct API interactions.

- **Release recording**: The rendered manifests and relevant metadata are serialized and stored into the release Secret in the cluster namespace.

Each release version reflects a snapshot of this process, enabling Helm commands such as `helm rollback` to revert to prior versions by reapplying the stored manifests. This mechanism ensures reproducibility and consistency, linking declared configurations directly to active cluster resources.

State management in Helm extends to tracking the status of each release. Helm records discrete release states such as `deployed`, `failed`, `pending-upgrade`, and others, encapsulated within the release Secret metadata. These states provide crucial feedback on the health and stage of the deployment, supporting nuanced operational workflows and troubleshooting.

It is important to distinguish between Helm's notion of release state and Kubernetes native state management. Helm manages the desired state through release manifests and tracks the success or failure of applying those manifests. Kubernetes, however, independently reconciles actual cluster state to declared desired state according to its controllers. This two-layered state model means that Helm must manage drift and rollback by effectively reapplying previous manifests or upgrades, while Kubernetes continuously converges resources toward the declared specifications.

Moreover, because charts are often parameterized to include conditional resource inclusion, the relationship between values and the rendered resources can be complex. Small changes in value configurations may result in significant differences in the generated manifests and thus in the resulting Kubernetes objects. Helm's release versioning captures these changes granularly, making it possible to audit configuration evolution over time.

From a design standpoint, Helm's model of releases as versioned, cluster-persisted entities provides a robust and flexible mechanism for application lifecycle management. It reconciles the imperative experience of applying manifests with the declarative nature of Kubernetes. This release-oriented approach empowers teams to manage application configurations systematically across environments with full history, traceability, and rollback capabilities.

In summary, Helm releases function as encapsulated, versioned records of all information required to define an application's deployment in Kubernetes. The interplay between charts, values, and Kubernetes resources, combined with persistent state storage in the cluster, enables Helm to manage and track release states with precision. This cohesive model underpins Helm's ability to provide repeatable, auditable, and flexible application delivery in complex Kubernetes environments.

5.2. Installation Workflows: Strategies and Best Practices

Effective installation workflows for Helm charts are foundational to leveraging Kubernetes package management with confidence, repeatability, and robustness. This discussion delves into crucial operational mechanisms—dry runs, dependency resolution, and idempotency—that underpin reliable chart deployments in both simple and complex environments. Emphasizing automation, each element contributes significantly to stable, predictable releases.

A dry run emulates the installation process without making persistent changes to the target cluster. Executing `helm install --dry-run` simulates rendering templates and validating manifests, providing critical insight into output resources and potential errors prior to deployment. By analyzing the configuration and resource manifests produced, developers and operators can preemptively identify misconfigurations or incompatibilities. Consider the following example where a chart is validated against the cluster API:

```
helm install my-release my-chart --dry-run --debug
```

This command performs template rendering, yielding annotated YAML manifests and diagnostic messages. The `--debug` flag exposes deeper details useful for troubleshooting. Dry runs are integral to continuous integration pipelines, enabling automated chart validation before committing to actual deployment, thus reducing the risk of failed upgrades or broken installations.

Dependency resolution within Helm charts manages the relationships and version constraints between charts and their subcharts. Each chart may specify dependencies in its `Chart.yaml`, necessitating correct fetching, versioning, and chart layer compositing. Failure to resolve dependencies accurately leads to incomplete or inconsistent installations. The `helm dependency update` command synchronizes and retrieves dependencies, ensuring the `charts/` directory is populated accordingly:

```
helm dependency update
```

Dependency resolution must be deterministic to guarantee reproducibility. To that end, charts should pin specific versions and use checksums for artifacts. This practice avoids drift in transitive dependencies, which can subtly alter behavior between installs. Moreover, charts distributed via repositories benefit from caching via local `helm repo update` synchronization, mitigating network-related variability.

A critical characteristic of installation workflows is idempotency—where repeated applications of a chart yield the same cluster state without unintended side effects. Helm ensures this by tracking release metadata in the cluster through ConfigMaps or Secrets in the `kube-system` namespace. Running `helm install` on an existing release triggers an error; in contrast, `helm upgrade --install` performs an atomic idempotent operation that installs the release if absent or upgrades it if present:

```
helm upgrade --install my-release my-chart
```

This pattern simplifies automation, enabling infrastructure-as-code workflows where the desired state is declaratively re-applied. Idempotency mitigates drift and supports continuous delivery by ensuring failed deployments can be re-attempted cleanly. Operators should design charts with idempotent hooks and resource management to ensure that updates do not result in resource duplication or orphaned artifacts.

Automation elements integrate these foundational strategies into robust pipelines. For instance, a typical Helm deployment pipeline might begin with a dry run to validate manifests, followed by dependency resolution to ensure all subcharts are up to date, and culminate with an `upgrade --install` command that applies the final release. Tooling such as Helmfile or Flux CD further orchestrates these steps declaratively, maintaining releases in a GitOps fashion.

Rigorous management of values and environment-specific configurations enhances repeatability. Helm supports `values.yaml` layering, enabling separation of base parameters and environment overrides. Combining this with version control and templating facilitates multiple deployments of the same chart across disparate environments with predictable outcomes. Incorporating checksum verification on values files and manifests can trigger automated rollbacks or alerts when drift is detected.

Ultimately, best practices include:

- Consistent use of `helm dependency update` prior to installation to ensure deterministic dependencies.

- Integration of dry runs with `--debug` to catch template and validation errors early.

- Employing `helm upgrade --install` for idempotent deployment and continuous delivery compatibility.

- Structuring charts and hooks to avoid side effects and facilitate clean upgrades.

- Managing and versioning values files alongside charts for controlled, environment-specific configurations.

- Embedding Helm workflows within automation pipelines and GitOps frameworks to achieve repeatability and auditability.

This synthesis of dry-run validation, dependable dependency handling, and idempotent deployment unlocks the full power and reliability of Helm for modern Kubernetes application lifecycle management. By applying these strategies methodically, engineers can ensure installations are repeatable, resilient to failure, and amenable to continuous automation.

5.3. Upgrade Patterns and Zero-Downtime Rollouts

Modern cloud-native applications necessitate continuous deployment practices that minimize service disruption while delivering new features and improvements. Achieving zero-downtime during upgrades is critical, particularly in systems where high availability and reliability are mandated by business requirements. Two pervasive upgrade strategies designed to fulfill these criteria are *blue/green deployments* and *canary releases*. Both approaches enable controlled rollout of new software versions, mitigate risks associated with updates, and underpin progressive delivery principles.

Blue/green deployment involves maintaining two separate but identically configured environments: the *blue* environment represents the live production system running the current stable release, whereas the *green* environment hosts the new version undergoing validation. Once the green environment is ready and tested, traffic is redirected almost instantaneously from blue to green. This traffic switch is typically implemented at the reverse proxy, load balancer, or ingress controller layer, enabling an atomic transition that is transparent to end users. Should issues arise post-cutover, a simple rollback to the blue environment restores the previous stable state without downtime.

A typical orchestration of blue/green deployment in Kubernetes involves deploying two sets of pods and services, one for each version, and updating the service selector or ingress routing accordingly. This strategy ensures no overlaps in state or configuration, preserving deployment immutability. However, it can be resource-intensive because of duplicated infrastructure during the transition period.

Conversely, **canary deployments** introduce newer versions gradually to a subset of users or requests, enabling real-time monitoring and validation under actual workload conditions before full release. This controlled exposure reduces risk by limiting the blast radius of potential defects or regressions. Canary patterns are especially suitable for data-intensive applications where unforeseen behaviors under production traffic can occur.

Canary rollout typically involves incrementally shifting traffic percentages to pods of the new version. Automated monitoring tools and metrics determine whether the upgrade meets predefined health and performance criteria. If anomalies are detected, the deployment can be halted or rolled back. This approach supports finer control but requires sophisticated traffic routing and telemetry integration.

Helm, as a powerful Kubernetes package manager, facilitates these upgrade patterns by providing robust mechanisms for managing application releases. Helm's release management capabilities simplify versioning, rollback, and configuration management, forming a foundation for progressive delivery.

Helm's `upgrade` command performs atomic updates to a release by comparing last deployed manifests with updated charts and applying changes through Kubernetes APIs. This declarative approach ensures that changes are applied consistently without manual intervention. Helm stores release information as Kubernetes secrets or ConfigMaps, enabling reliable state tracking.

While Helm provides the mechanism for applying updates, zero-downtime deployments require careful chart design and orchestration. For example, readiness and liveness probes in pod specifications allow Kubernetes to manage rolling updates by detecting pod health and ensuring new pods serve traffic only when ready. Helm charts can define `strategy` parameters within `Deployment` manifests to leverage Kubernetes native `RollingUpdate` capabilities.

```
spec:
  strategy:
    type: RollingUpdate
    rollingUpdate:
      maxUnavailable: 0
```

```
    maxSurge: 1
```

This configuration enforces zero downtime by only updating one pod at a time with no reduction in available replicas.

Beyond native rolling updates, Helm can integrate with advanced progressive delivery controllers such as Argo Rollouts or Flagger. These tools extend Kubernetes with canary and blue/green deployment capabilities, offering automated traffic shifting, metrics analysis, and rollback automation based on live telemetry.

Flagger orchestrates canary deployment by managing traffic routes via service mesh providers or ingress controllers and monitoring application metrics defined as Kubernetes `Prometheus` alerts. A typical Flagger resource references a Helm release and configures a canary strategy:

```
apiVersion: flagger.app/v1beta1
kind: Canary
metadata:
  name: myapp
spec:
  targetRef:
    apiVersion: apps/v1
    kind: Deployment
    name: myapp
  service:
    port: 80
  canaryAnalysis:
    interval: 1m
    threshold: 10
    metrics:
    - name: request-success-rate
      threshold: 99
    webhooks:
    - name: load-test
      type: pre-rollout
      url: http://loadtester.test.svc.cluster.local
```

With this integration, Helm serves as the declarative configuration layer, while Flagger manages safe progressive delivery, including automated promotion and rollback.

In the domain of blue/green deployments, Helm charts can be parameterized to deploy separate environments by dynamically setting labels, service selectors, and ingress rules. Switchovers occur by updating a Kubernetes service or ingress to point to either the blue or green version without modifying pod specifications directly. This facilitates rapid environment swaps without manual intervention.

Zero-downtime rollouts embody a combination of Kubernetes primitives, Helm-based release management, and advanced deployment strategies to meet evolving application delivery demands. Blue/green deployments provide a clear cutover between stable and new versions, ensuring quick rollback capabilities, at the cost of resource duplication. Canary deployments focus on minimizing risk through incremental traffic shifts and observation of live metrics, albeit requiring more sophisticated orchestration.

The modularity of Helm charts, combined with Kubernetes native capabilities and progressive delivery tools, makes it feasible to implement both strategies with minimal operational complexity. Effective upgrade patterns thus empower engineering teams to deliver continuous innovation safely, maintaining user experience continuity and operational resilience.

5.4. Rollback Mechanisms and Failure Recovery

In container orchestration and Kubernetes application lifecycle management, Helm stands out as a powerful tool to simplify deployments. However, the inherent complexity of distributed systems, combined with frequent updates and configuration changes, mandates robust rollback mechanisms and failure recovery strategies. Helm's capabilities in this dimension ensure that administrators and operators can reliably navigate failures, minimize downtime, and maintain system integrity.

Helm uses the concept of *releases* to track each deployment of a chart. Each release embodies a specific state, including the chart version, configuration values, and rendered Kubernetes manifests. This state tracking is fundamental to rollback and recovery processes. When an upgrade or installation command is executed, Helm creates a new release version, maintaining a history that enables restoring prior states seamlessly.

Rollback in Helm is initiated via the `helm rollback` command, which reverts a release to a previous revision by reinstalling the corresponding manifests and state. Conceptually, this process treats each release as a snapshot, allowing restoration to any known good configuration recorded in the history. Internally, Helm retrieves the revision to be rolled back from its storage backend (typically ConfigMaps or Secrets in the cluster's namespace) and performs a deployment akin to an upgrade using the old manifests and values.

This rollback operation incorporates several important aspects:

- **Idempotency:** The rollback command ensures that repeated executions produce consistent cluster states. It redeploys resources with the exact configurations of the target revision, overwriting divergent changes caused by failed or partial upgrades.

- **State Preservation:** The rollback does not discard the failed or intermediate releases. Instead, the revision history remains intact, allowing multiple successive rollbacks and forward rollbacks (upgrades) as needed.

- **Versioning:** Each rollback itself increments the release revision counter, preserving an audit trail and enabling traceability of changes through time.

Consider the following command to revert a release named `myapp` to revision 2:

```
helm rollback myapp 2
```

Helm will reapply the Kubernetes manifests stored with revision 2, restoring the application state as it was.

Failure recovery is complicated by stateful workloads and the presence of resources that have complex lifecycle semantics. StatefulSets, PersistentVolumeClaims (PVCs), and Custom Resource Definitions (CRDs) often require careful handling during rollback or failed upgrade scenarios to avoid data loss or inconsistent states.

Helm's design recognizes these challenges and provides mechanisms to manage stateful cleanup safely:

- **Hooks for Pre- and Post-Rollback:** Helm charts may define lifecycle hooks, such as `pre-rollback` and `post-rollback`, which allow custom preparations before the rollback or cleanup actions after rollback completes. For example, operators might pause traffic to a service, back up data volumes, or reconfigure dependent components.

- **Retains Persistent Data:** Helm does not delete PVCs or other non-templated, user-defined persistent resources during rollbacks to prevent data loss. It treats these resources as external to the release lifecycle, allowing manual intervention when necessary.

- **Selective Resource Replacement:** Helm differentiates between immutable resource fields and mutable ones. When rolling back, only the mutable fields of resources are updated, avoiding operations that Kubernetes restricts (such as volume size changes in PVCs).

By leveraging these mechanisms, Helm provides operators granular control over the sequence of actions during recovery, mitigating the risk of data corruption or unintended disruptions.

Despite Helm's automation and state tracking, complete failure recovery depends on several operational best practices to guarantee safe rollback and forward movement:

- **Release History Size Configuration:** Helm retains a configurable number of release revisions (default 10 in Helm 3). Operators should ensure sufficient history depth to accommodate multiple rollbacks, especially in high-frequency update environments.

- **Use of `--atomic` Flag:** Deployments using `--atomic` will fail the upgrade and automatically rollback if any step fails in the process. This ensures the cluster returns to a consistent state without manual intervention.

- **Validation and Testing of Manifests:** Pre-flight validation of manifests and values through tools such as `helm template` or third-party validators reduces the risk of introducing irrecoverable errors.

- **Explicit Hook Management:** Proper implementation of hooks must consider idempotency and side effects, as incorrect hooks can leave residual states that complicate rollback.

- **Monitoring and Alerting:** Integrating Helm deployments with monitoring tools to detect failed upgrades promptly allows rapid initiation of recovery procedures.

More intricate failure scenarios, such as partial cluster outages or manual resource manipulations, require advanced strategies:

- **Manual Resource Reconciliation:** Occasionally, Kubernetes resources might diverge from Helm's stored manifests due to out-of-band changes. Helm provides `helm diff` and `helm status` commands to detect discrepancies and guide corrective actions.

- **CRDs and Version Migrations:** When rollbacks involve CRD versions or schema changes, Helm does not automatically revert these kinds of resources to avoid cluster-wide instability. Instead, manual coordination and migration tooling are necessary.

- **Cluster State Snapshots:** Helm integrates effectively with external backup systems capturing etcd snapshots or persistent volumes, enabling full restoration of cluster states beyond Helm's own release tracking.

These considerations underscore that Helm is a vital component in the recovery toolkit, but operators must combine it with Kubernetes-native features and organizational policies to design comprehensive recovery frameworks.

Rollback mechanisms and failure recovery in Helm are founded on rigorous state management, revision tracking, and extensible hooks to enable safe and reliable deployments. By providing engineered pathways to revert releases and preserve critical state, Helm reduces operational risk in dynamic environments. Thoughtful application of Helm's rollback features, coupled with contextual understanding of the managed workloads and infrastructure, is essential to ensure resilient Kubernetes application delivery.

5.5. Release History, Revision Management, and Drift Detection

Effective management of infrastructure and application configurations in dynamic environments demands rigorous tracking of release histories, precise revision control, and proactive detection of configuration drift. These capabilities are foundational to establishing traceability, ensuring consistency, and enabling rapid remediation, thereby maintaining system integrity throughout the lifecycle.

Tracking and Visualizing Release Histories

Release history encapsulates the chronological record of deployments and configuration states applied to a system. Capturing this history facilitates auditing, postmortem analyses, and compliance verification. An effective release history management process involves capturing not only version identifiers but also metadata such as deployment timestamps, authorship, detailed change lists, applied policies, and environmental contexts.

Visualization tools, often based on graph structures or timelines, significantly enhance comprehension of release progression and interdependencies. For example, directed acyclic graphs (DAGs) can represent successive states and branching deployment paths, providing immediate insight into parallel releases or rollback points. This visualization aids operators and engineers in identifying at which point a functional or performance regression may have been introduced.

Technologies such as GitOps implement continuous synchronization between declarative configuration repositories and target environments, inherently maintaining a detailed release history. Each commit in a repository corresponds to a specific configuration or application state, automatically traceable and reversible. Additionally, augmenting release history with annotations from monitoring and incident management systems enhances the narrative context, linking configuration changes directly with observed system behavior.

Historical Revision Management

Revision management involves the systematic recording, storage, and retrieval of configuration versions or application code states, supporting the principles of change control and versioning. Unlike source code version control alone, infrastructure revision management must account for binary artifacts, configuration files, and stateful metadata.

Using immutable, content-addressed storage for revisions ensures integrity and reproducibility. Each revision is typically identified by cryptographic hashes (e.g., SHA-256) that guarantee artifact uniqueness and detect unauthorized alterations. Coupling this with signed commits or tags provides authentication assurance critical for regulated environments.

The revision management system should support branching and merging semantics to accommodate multi-environment workflows (development, staging, production) and parallel feature development. Employing semantic versioning standards facilitates meaningful release increments, enabling stakeholders to interpret the impact and priority of changes effectively.

Automated integration of revision metadata into deployment pipelines allows for deterministic rollbacks, where reverting to a known-good state is not only feasible but also rapid and reliable. Maintaining detailed changelogs and release notes linked to revisions assists in incident response and knowledge transfer.

Configuration Drift and Its Detection

Configuration drift occurs when the actual state of a system deviates from its desired or declared state. Drift can arise due to manual changes, software updates, hardware failures, or environment-specific adaptations, leading to inconsistencies that complicate troubleshooting and introduce security vulnerabilities.

Drift detection mechanisms operate by continuously comparing the live configuration against the authoritative source of truth-usually a declarative configuration store or infrastructure-as-code repository. This comparison can leverage state snapshotting, hash comparisons, or direct API queries to infrastructure components.

Techniques for drift detection fall into two main categories:

- **Passive detection:** Periodic scanning of deployed resources, followed by differential analysis against the declared configuration. This approach trades immediacy for resource efficiency.

- **Active enforcement:** Utilizing agents or controllers that intercept or reject unauthorized changes in real time, effectively preventing drift rather than merely detecting it.

Advanced drift detection incorporates semantic understanding, recognizing that some state differences might be immaterial or transient (e.g., timestamps, ephemeral IP addresses). Anomaly scoring or heuristic filters help reduce false positives, focusing operator attention on meaningful divergences.

Integration with alerting and remediation workflows is crucial. Upon detecting drift, orchestration frameworks can trigger automated remediation policies, reverting resources to their desired state and thus closing the control loop. This ensures the environment remains consistent with organizational policies without requiring manual intervention.

Synthesis to Ensure Operational Transparency

Combining these three pillars-release history visualization, rigorous revision management, and continuous drift detection-establishes a comprehensive framework for operational transparency. This framework ensures that engineering teams always know precisely what is running, why it is running, and how each state was achieved.

This knowledge enables confident decision-making during incident response, capacity planning, and regulatory audits. Moreover, it supports best practices such as immutable infrastructure, where each deployment is a fresh instantiation of a versioned artifact rather than an incremental patch, thereby minimizing untracked state changes.

Ultimately, robust release and revision management paired with proactive drift detection forms the backbone of resilient, scalable, and secure infrastructure automation. It empowers organizations to maintain a declarative, self-healing model of their environments, minimizing human error and accelerating the velocity of reliable software delivery.

5.6. Automated Remediation and Health Probes

A cornerstone of modern resilient systems is the capacity to automatically detect and remediate failures with minimal human intervention. This capability hinges fundamentally on the integration of health checks, readiness probes, and post-deployment hooks. Together, these mechanisms enable rapid identification of service degradation or failures and facilitate self-healing actions that maintain system integrity and availability.

Health checks serve as primary indicators of application and infrastructure status. They typically encompass two complementary types: *liveness probes*, which determine if an application is alive and running, and *readiness probes*, which assess whether the application is prepared to serve requests. By programmatically querying these endpoints, orchestrators and service meshes gain real-time visibility into operational conditions, triggering corrective measures when anomalies are detected.

Liveness probes frequently monitor critical processes, resource availability, or responsiveness to essential commands. For example, a liveness probe may execute a diagnostic script returning success only if the application's main thread and dependent services are functioning correctly. Should the probe fail, orchestration platforms such as Kubernetes consider the container unhealthy and initiate a restart, mitigating prolonged outages.

Readiness probes, on the other hand, often verify initialization sequences, configuration loading, dependency connections, or cache warming. Their primary function is to gate traffic delivery, ensuring that requests are routed only to components that are fully prepared, thereby preventing error propagation and degraded user experience.

Effective readiness probes need to balance thoroughness with efficiency. Overly complex probes introduce latency and may result in false negatives, whereas superficial checks risk masking subtle failures. Best practices recommend that readiness probes focus on the minimum subset of conditions essential for correct request processing. For instance, rather than performing exhaustive database integrity checks, a readiness probe might verify connectivity to the primary data store and successful authentication.

In container orchestration environments, readiness probes are typically implemented as HTTP endpoints, TCP socket checks, or command executions. For example, an HTTP GET request returning status 200 indicates readiness, whereas a non-200 response signals the need to withhold traffic routing. The following sample configuration snippet illustrates an HTTP readiness probe specification within Kubernetes:

```
readinessProbe:
  httpGet:
    path: /health/ready
    port: 8080
  initialDelaySeconds: 10
  periodSeconds: 5
  failureThreshold: 3
```

This configuration instructs the Kubernetes scheduler to begin readiness checks 10 seconds after container startup, polling every 5 seconds, and marking the container as unready if three consecutive failures occur.

Post-deployment hooks complement health probes by automating actions immediately following software release or infrastructure changes. These hooks can validate post-deployment conditions, execute remedial scripts, or trigger rollbacks in case of detected failures. Integration with continuous deployment pipelines enables rapid mitigation of deployment-related defects, reducing mean time to recovery (MTTR).

Typical post-deploy hooks include sanity checks to confirm system responsiveness, performance benchmarks to detect regressions, and configuration validations to ensure environment consistency. In complex microservices architectures, deploying post-deploy hooks that query multiple interdependent services can identify partial failures that are not apparent in isolated health probes.

Implementation of post-deploy remediation hooks can employ declarative infrastructure as code frameworks or container lifecycle management features. For example, Kubernetes supports `postStart` and `preStop` hooks within container lifecycle events:

```
lifecycle:
  postStart:
    exec:
      command: ["/bin/sh", "-c", "/opt/scripts/postdeploy-check.
      sh"]
```

This hook executes a custom script after container creation, enabling verification or adjustment procedures vital for a healthy deployment.

Integrating health checks, readiness probes, and post-deploy hooks achieves a robust feedback loop, where detection and remediation processes are tightly coupled. Anomalies discovered by probes prompt orchestration or management layers to invoke post-deploy hooks or automated restart policies, expediting recovery and limiting exposure to degraded states.

For instance, if a readiness probe fails repeatedly after deployment, a post-deploy hook may trigger a rollback of the service version or adjust resource allocation dynamically. Likewise, liveness failures can induce container termination and recreation, with readiness gates ensuring that new instances do not receive traffic until fully operational.

This layered automation supports graceful degradation strategies, allowing partial service availability while failed components are remediated. Additionally, it facilitates predictive maintenance when health metrics are correlated over time, enabling preemptive interventions before failures manifest.

While automation substantially reduces manual intervention, careful design considerations must be applied. Overly aggressive failure detection settings may cause unnecessary restarts, leading to instability or cascading failures. Conversely, lenient thresholds can delay remediation, allowing errors to impact users.

Moreover, health probes and hooks should be secured and resilient to avoid becoming attack vectors or single points of failure. Implementing authentication for probe endpoints, rate-limiting checks, and proper isolation of remediation scripts are critical safeguards.

Consistency across environments is essential; idiosyncratic probe implementations can complicate troubleshooting and reduce toolchain interoperability. Standardizing probes and hook templates, combined with comprehensive logging and observability, enhances reliability and facilitates root cause analysis.

The integrated workflow typically unfolds in the following steps:

1. On deployment, post-deploy hooks execute validation and remedial scripts to ensure baseline health.

2. Readiness probes continuously assess operational readiness, controlling traffic routing to avoid degraded instances.

3. Liveness probes monitor ongoing application health, triggering automatic restarts upon failure detection.

4. Orchestration platforms respond to probe failures by evicting unhealthy instances and initiating remediation sequences.

5. Historical probe data is ingested into monitoring systems to inform predictive analytics and incident response planning.

This tightly coupled approach to automated detection and remediation forms the foundation of resilient, self-healing infrastructure, enabling rapid recovery and improved service reliability with minimal human overhead.

Chapter 6

Helm Chart Repository Management and Distribution

A well-managed Helm chart repository is the linchpin of scalable, collaborative Kubernetes deployments. This chapter uncovers the mechanics and strategies behind securely publishing, organizing, and distributing charts, ensuring your software supply chain is both efficient and trustworthy. From cryptographic signing to automated CI/CD publishing, you'll learn how to turn chart repositories into a robust foundation for reliable application delivery.

6.1. Chart Repository Formats and Protocols

A Helm chart repository serves as a structured distribution point for Helm charts, enabling streamlined package management in Kubernetes environments. Its architecture hinges on well-defined formats, directory layouts, indexing mechanisms, and standardized protocols, primarily HTTP(S), to facilitate reliable and efficient chart retrieval. Understanding these components is critical for developing, hosting, and interacting with Helm repositories.

At its core, a Helm chart repository is a web-accessible directory containing packaged charts and an index file that catalogues these charts. The packaged chart is an archive-a compressed tarball-with a `.tgz` extension. Each such package encapsulates all necessary Kubernetes resource templates, metadata, and dependencies required to deploy an application or service.

Directory Layout and File Format

A typical Helm repository comprises a root directory hosting the essential files:

- `index.yaml`: The primary index file enumerating all available chart versions.

- Chart package files: The `.tgz` archives, each named according to the convention `<chart-name>-<version>.tgz`.

Unlike conventional layered directory structures, the repository itself is usually flat, with chart archive files colocated in a single directory alongside the index. However, repositories can be encapsulated within web servers that present the directory abstractly over HTTP(S).

The chart package structure inside each `.tgz` archive follows a specific hierarchy:

```
<chart-name>/
```

130

```
Chart.yaml      # Metadata about the chart (name, version,
   dependencies)
values.yaml     # Default configuration values
charts/         # Subcharts (dependencies) packaged within
templates/      # Kubernetes manifests templates
README.md       # Optional documentation
```

This organization ensures that Helm clients can parse and expand charts predictably, adhering to the conventions specified in the Helm Chart Schema.

Indexing Mechanism

The index.yaml file acts as a centralized catalog of the repository contents. It is a YAML-formatted manifest automatically generated by Helm tools (e.g., helm repo index) and contains metadata about each chart version present in the repository.

Structurally, index.yaml includes:

- apiVersion: The version of the index format, currently v1.

- entries: A mapping from chart names to a list of version descriptors.

- generated: A timestamp marking the generation time of the index.

Each entry for a chart version consists of metadata fields such as version number, description, keywords, API versions, home URL, and crucially, the URLs where the package can be accessed. These URLs are relative or absolute pointers to the chart archives, enabling clients to fetch them on demand.

An excerpt of index.yaml content is exemplified below:

```
apiVersion: v1
generated: 2024-04-27T12:34:56Z
entries:
  my-application:
  - version: 1.0.3
    appVersion: "2.0.0"
```

```
    description: A sample application chart
    urls:
    - my-application-1.0.3.tgz
    digest: sha256:abc123...
  - version: 1.0.4
    appVersion: "2.1.0"
    description: Updated with new features
    urls:
    - my-application-1.0.4.tgz
    digest: sha256:def456...
```

The presence of checksums (via `digest`) offers integrity verification for downloaded charts.

Protocols Underlying Chart Distribution

Chart repositories are predominantly served over HTTP or HTTPS protocols. The use of HTTPS is strongly recommended to guarantee confidentiality and integrity during transmission. Helm clients interact with these repositories following HTTP-based conventions.

When adding a repository, the Helm client requires the base URL pointing to the repository root, where the `index.yaml` file resides. The client fetches this index file to obtain a list of available charts and their corresponding versions. Subsequently, charts are downloaded by accessing the URLs specified within the index.

The interaction workflow involves:

- Index retrieval: The client performs an HTTP GET request for the `index.yaml` file.

- Chart resolution: Parsing the index to resolve a chart name and version.

- Package download: Performing an HTTP GET request for the corresponding `.tgz` archive.

- Validation and unpacking: The client verifies checksums (if present) before extracting the chart.

Helm clients support standard HTTP behaviors including redirects and caching headers, allowing repositories hosted via content delivery networks (CDNs), static web servers, or specialized Helm repository services.

Advanced Indexing and Multi-Repository Support

Helm supports repository aggregation and index merging, enabling multiple repositories to be combined. The index file format and tooling allow merging multiple index.yaml files into a new, unified one, facilitating multi-source chart discovery.

Moreover, the index can contain URLs that reference charts hosted on separate domains or storage backends, enabling federated repositories. This flexibility, together with the flat directory structure, simplifies repository maintenance and scaling.

Alternative Chart Distribution Formats and Protocols

While the HTTP(S)-based repository remains canonical, alternatives exist:

- OCI (Open Container Initiative) registries: Helm charts can now be stored as OCI artifacts in container registries, using the OCI Distribution Specification. This method leverages the container ecosystem's content-addressable storage and standardized protocols such as HTTPS with token-based authentication.

- Git repositories: Helm charts can be distributed via Git by pointing the Helm client to raw archive files or utilizing GitOps tools, but this approach lacks the indexing and metadata richness of a standard repository.

Nonetheless, the traditional Helm repository format, characterized by the index.yaml and .tgz archives served over HTTP(S), remains widely adopted due to its simplicity, tooling support, and compatibility with existing infrastructure.

The Helm chart repository's structured interplay of flat directory layouts, a centralized YAML index, and HTTP(S) transport protocols establishes a robust framework for chart distribution. Understanding its anatomy enables efficient management, extension, and integration of Helm repositories within Kubernetes-centric continuous delivery pipelines.

6.2. Publishing and Versioning Charts

Effective management of Helm charts requires a systematic approach to packaging, versioning, and distribution. This section elaborates on practical workflows to package charts, manage semantic versioning, update repository indices, and release charts to local and remote repositories for broad consumption.

Packaging a Helm chart creates a distributable archive that streamlines deployment and version control. A chart package is a compressed .tgz file encapsulating all chart files, including templates, dependencies, and metadata.

To package a chart:

```
helm package /path/to/chart
```

This command creates a package in the current directory named following the format chart-name-version.tgz, where version corresponds to the version specified in the Chart.yaml manifest. It is prudent to validate chart syntax and templates via helm lint before packaging to ensure quality.

Semantic Versioning (SemVer) is critical to manage chart evolution, signal breaking changes, and maintain compatibility with dependent systems. The versioning scheme follows the pattern MAJOR.MINOR.PATCH:

- **MAJOR**: Introduces incompatible API changes or architecture modifications.

- **MINOR**: Adds backward-compatible functionality or features.

- **PATCH**: Applies backward-compatible bug fixes or minor improvements.

The `Chart.yaml` file governs the chart version through the `version` key. Chart authors should increment these numbers according to the nature of changes between releases. Additionally, the `appVersion` metadata key specifies the version of the application the chart installs and is typically independent of the chart's own versioning.

Example snippet from `Chart.yaml`:

```
apiVersion: v2
name: my-application
version: 1.3.2
appVersion: 2.4.1
```

Adhering strictly to SemVer semantics enables automated tooling to determine upgrade paths and compatibility.

A Helm chart repository requires an updated index file (`index.yaml`) that catalogs all available charts and their versions, metadata, and URLs to package archives. After successfully packaging one or more charts, the repository index must be refreshed.

Consider a repository directory structure as follows:

```
charts/
  myapp-1.3.2.tgz
  anotherapp-0.9.5.tgz
index.yaml
```

To update the index file, use:

135

```
helm repo index ./charts --url https://example.com/charts
```

Here, --url specifies the base URL where the chart packages will be served. The command scans the directory for all .tgz packages, generates the index.yaml with relevant checksums and metadata, and writes it to the directory.

It is essential to serve the index.yaml and the packaged charts over HTTP or HTTPS, ensuring consistent URLs that clients use for chart discovery and downloads.

Using a local file server or directory, users can test chart consumption workflows. To add a local repository, run:

```
helm repo add local-charts file:///absolute/path/to/charts
helm repo update
```

This makes the charts discoverable to Helm consumers via the alias local-charts. Chart installation commands can now reference this repository name.

For broader distribution, charts must be uploaded to remote artifact repositories or Helm chart hosting services such as ChartMuseum, GitHub Pages, Artifactory, or cloud-specific solutions.

A typical workflow for publishing involves the following steps:

- **Package the chart** locally, ensuring proper version increment.

- **Upload the package** to the remote repository storage location, e.g., an object store bucket or HTTP server.

- **Update the repository index** on the remote server with the new chart entry.

When repositories support artifact upload over API or CLI, the process can be scripted. Using ChartMuseum CLI as an example:

```
cm-push myapp-1.3.2.tgz --host https://charts.example.com
```

Alternatively, hosting charts on GitHub Pages combines artifact storage and automatic version control provided by Git. Using GitHub Actions, automated workflows can package charts, update the `index.yaml`, and push changes, facilitating continuous delivery of charts.

After successful publishing, users add or update the repository reference:

```
helm repo add example-repo https://charts.example.com
helm repo update
```

When releasing new chart versions, old versions must remain accessible for reproducibility; hence, chart repositories typically store all historical versions unless explicitly deprecated.

The `deprecated` field in `Chart.yaml` or repository metadata signals to clients that a version should no longer be used for new deployments due to critical issues or obsolescence:

```
apiVersion: v2
name: my-application
version: 2.0.0
deprecated: true
```

Tools and users may utilize deprecation notices to guide upgrade strategies. Removing chart versions from a remote repository requires explicit action and can impact users relying on those releases, so it must be managed carefully.

- Always increment the chart version following SemVer guidelines after any change to the chart or its dependencies.

- Use automated CI/CD pipelines to package, lint, and publish charts to prevent human errors.

- Secure remote repositories with authentication and authorization to prevent unauthorized chart publishing.

- Regularly synchronize and update repository indexes following every chart addition or removal.

- Document deprecation policies and provide clear upgrade paths to end users.

- Test chart installations from remote repositories to validate integrity and accessibility.

Adhering to these workflows ensures reliable chart distribution, consistent version tracking, and smoother upgrades, thereby enhancing the overall reliability and maintainability of Kubernetes deployments.

6.3. Repository Authentication, Signing, and Provenance

Cryptographic signing, provenance tracking, and repository authentication form the foundational pillars of secure and traceable software distribution, particularly in environments reliant on containerized applications and Helm charts. Mastery of these techniques ensures that software artifacts maintain integrity, authenticity, and verifiable origins throughout their lifecycle, significantly mitigating supply chain security risks.

Cryptographic Signing of Charts

Signing a chart involves creating a digital signature that binds the chart's content to the identity of its creator. This process provides a mechanism to detect tampering and to verify the publisher's authenticity. The signing workflow generally employs asymmetric cryptography, where a private key generates a signature for the chart package, and the corresponding public key is used by consumers to verify it.

The widely adopted standard for Helm charts is to generate a `.prov` provenance file alongside the packaged chart using `helm package --sign`. The signature employs OpenPGP standards, encapsulating a hash of the chart's contents.

```
helm package mychart/ --sign --key "mykey" --keyring ~/.gnupg/
    pubring.kbx
```

This command produces two files: `mychart-1.0.0.tgz` and `mychart-1.0.0.tgz.prov`. The `.prov` file contains metadata, including the signing key's fingerprint, the timestamp of signing, and a cryptographic digest of the chart contents.

Verification of a signed chart requires the public key that corresponds to the signer's private key to be present in the user's keyring. The verification process affirms that the chart has remained unaltered and that its origin matches the trusted key.

```
helm verify mychart-1.0.0.tgz
```

If the signature is invalid, missing, or untrusted, the verification will fail, preventing inadvertent deployment of unauthorized artifacts.

Managing Provenance Files

Provenance files serve as cryptographically verifiable certificates of authenticity and integrity. Beyond mere signature data, they encapsulate rich metadata including chart dependencies, maintainers, version information, and the hashing algorithm employed. This metadata enables operations such as automated dependency checks, audit logging, and traceability across distributed repositories.

Effective management of provenance involves secure storage of these files, integration with Continuous Integration/Continuous Deployment (CI/CD) pipelines for automatic signing, and retention policies that maintain their availability for verification throughout the artifact's lifecycle. The `.prov` file format, based on in-toto standards, is extensible and allows embedding of additional attestations, such as build environment details or vulnerability scan results, strengthening the trust chain.

Provenance metadata can be programmatically extracted and verified as part of automated workflows to ensure that only artifacts with verifiable and trusted provenance are deployed.

Verifying Trusted Origins

Verification of trusted origins hinges on establishing a robust trust model anchored in well-managed cryptographic keys and trust policies. Common approaches include:

- **Key Distribution and Trust Anchors**: Public keys must be distributed via secure channels, often using key servers, metadata repositories, or organizational PKI infrastructures. Trust anchors (root keys) form the basis upon which signatures are validated.

- **Key Expiry and Revocation**: Keys should incorporate expiration and be subject to revocation mechanisms to mitigate risks of key compromise. Revocation lists or online status protocols provide real-time assurance of key validity.

- **Chain of Trust**: In environments with multiple signers or tiers (for example, upstream maintainers and downstream integrators), chain-of-trust models require validating intermediate signatures against trusted root keys.

Consumers of Helm charts or other packaged artifacts must enforce strict verification policies reflecting the organizational risk appetite, ensuring that every accepted signature is both cryptographically sound and rooted in an approved trust anchor.

Authenticating Repository Access

Authentication to repositories extends the security posture by controlling who can publish, retrieve, and modify artifacts. Common industry best practices include:

- **TLS/SSL Encryption**: Transport-level encryption via TLS secures communications against interception and man-in-the-middle attacks.

- **Token-Based Authentication**: OAuth2 tokens, JWTs (JSON Web Tokens), or API keys allow fine-grained access control, often integrated with identity providers or external authentication systems.

- **Mutual TLS (mTLS)**: Mutual certificate authentication ensures both the client and server authenticate each other, significantly elevating trust in highly sensitive environments.

- **Role-Based Access Control (RBAC)**: Access privileges scoped by roles ensure that only authorized users can perform sensitive repository operations such as pushing new charts or deleting existing ones.

When deploying Helm repositories, maintainers should leverage repository servers that support strong authentication mechanisms. For example, integrating with `ChartMuseum` or OCI-compliant artifact registries enables enhanced access control alongside Helm chart hosting.

Authentication credentials must be securely managed, rotated regularly, and audited, as repository compromise can enable unauthorized distribution of malicious artifacts.

Integrating Signing and Authentication for End-to-End Security

The combination of cryptographic chart signing, verified provenance, trusted origin validation, and stringent repository authentication establishes a layered security model. This multi-faceted approach ensures that:

- Only authorized entities sign and upload charts,

- Artifacts retrieved are verifiably untampered and originate from trusted sources,

- Access to repositories is tightly controlled to prevent unauthorized modifications.

Automated CI/CD pipelines can enforce signing policies and provenance verification at every stage, while deployment agents verify signatures and provenance files before installation, promoting both security and traceability.

The established cryptographic guarantees also facilitate compliance auditing and forensic analysis, enabling organizations to trace a deployed artifact back through its creation and distribution chain, drastically reducing the attack surface of the software supply chain.

6.4. Organizing Chart Repositories for Scale

At the heart of scaling Helm chart management lies the challenge of structuring repositories to accommodate multiple teams, diverse products, and varied deployment environments. Effective organization must support maintainability, foster reuse, and enable rapid, parallel development without bottlenecks or friction. This section outlines best practices synthesized from practical industry approaches, adapting principles of modularity, versioning, and governance to Helm chart repositories.

A foundational decision is choosing the structural model that best fits organizational needs. The two predominant paradigms are monorepos and polyrepos, each with distinct trade-offs.

A monorepo consolidates all chart artifacts across teams, products, and environments under a single repository. This model simplifies dependency management and atomic changes across charts. Shared libraries and common chart templates can coexist, enabling easy code sharing and refactoring.

To maintain clarity in large monorepos, logical segmentation is critical. A common directory hierarchy might look like:

```
charts/
  core-infrastructure/
    redis/
    prometheus/
  product-a/
    frontend/
    backend/
  product-b/
    database/
    api/
environments/
  staging/
  production/
```

Each product or service maintains its subdirectory, with environment-specific deployment manifests kept separate but linked via versioned chart references. Using dedicated tooling to infer changes and manage chart dependencies facilitates faster CI/CD pipelines in large monorepos.

Alternatively, polyrepos isolate projects or components into distinct Git repositories. This model enhances autonomy for teams, aligns with microservices ownership, and reduces the risk of cross-product interference.

Polyrepo organization commonly matches team boundaries or product lines, such as:

```
helm-charts-product-a/
helm-charts-product-b/
helm-charts-common/
```

Shared components or base charts live in a separate common repository. Cross-repository dependencies must be carefully versioned and managed. While this approach requires additional coordination, it enables teams to independently evolve their charts with tailored lifecycle policies.

Regardless of the repository model, embracing chart modularity ensures scalability. Each chart should encapsulate a clear and limited scope: a microservice, a database, or a core infrastructure component. Reusing charts through dependencies and umbrella charts promotes DRY (Don't Repeat Yourself) principles and reduces maintenance overhead.

Key best practices include:

- **Use Chart Dependencies:** Define `requirements.yaml` or `Chart.yaml` dependencies to express hierarchical relationships, enabling independent versioning and updates.

- **Employ Library Charts:** Create charts that serve as libraries providing templates or helper functions to promote consistency across charts.

- **Encapsulate Configuration:** Separate configuration values per environment via distinct `values.yaml` files or overlays, ensuring environment-specific customization while reusing core templates.

A rigorous versioning scheme aligned with semantic versioning (SemVer) is indispensable for large-scale chart repositories. Consistent versioning mitigates dependency conflicts and supports repeatable builds.

Each chart follows its own version trajectory reflecting backward-compatible or breaking changes. This model is natural for polyrepos but also feasible in a monorepo when chart builds and releases are automated per component.

For some organizations, especially those managing tightly coupled products, synchronizing versions across charts simplifies dependency resolution and deployment consistency. Techniques such as coordinated multi-module releases or tooling like Helmfile can orchestrate synchronized deployments.

Automated pipeline integration ensures version bumping, linting, testing, packaging, and publishing charts to Helm repositories (e.g., ChartMuseum, OCI registries) are reliable and reproducible. Tagging and release automation reduce manual error and improve developer velocity.

Environments-development, staging, production-introduce complexity in maintaining divergent configurations and deployment policies. Strategies to address this include:

- **Environment-Specific Values Files:** Maintain separate `values-{env}.yaml` files alongside charts, applying them during Helm install or upgrade commands.

- **Overlays and Parametrization Tools:** Utilize tools such as Helmfile, Kustomize, or customized scripts to merge base charts with environment overlays, enabling declarative and reproducible deployment manifests.

- **Environment-Aware Chart Repositories:** Host private or public Helm repositories segmented by environment or lifecycle stage, restricting deployment access and promoting controlled promotion workflows.

Scaling chart repositories across organizations requires governance to enforce conventions, review changes, and manage security implications.

Document clear guidelines for chart structure, naming, versioning, and linting rules. Consistent formatting enhances readability and reduces onboarding friction.

Integrate chart changes into code review workflows, employing automated linting and security scanners to catch vulnerabilities or misconfigurations early. Enforce mandatory approvals and use branch protections to maintain repository integrity.

Segment access based on team responsibilities, ensuring least privilege principles. This reduces risk during deployments and accidental deletion or modification of critical charts.

Leveraging the ecosystem of Helm-related and GitOps tools streamlines managing chart repositories at scale:

- **Helmfile and Helm-3:** Facilitate declarative management of multiple charts and their values, enhancing reproducibility.

- **Chart Repositories:** Use robust chart repository solutions supporting index file caching, signing, and artifact storage.

- **CI/CD Pipelines:** Automate chart linting, testing, packaging, and publication to reduce human error and accelerate delivery cycles.

- **Dependency and Version Management:** Employ tools like Renovate or Dependabot to automate dependency updates with pull requests.

Organizing Helm chart repositories for scale mandates deliberate structure, embracing modularity, automation, and governance. Tailoring repository models to organizational topology and product complexity, while investing in tooling and standards, unlocks maintainable and agile large-scale development.

6.5. Automated Chart Publishing in CI/CD Pipelines

The integration of chart packaging, validation, and deployment processes within continuous integration and continuous delivery (CI/CD) pipelines is pivotal for accelerating development velocity while ensuring the consistency and reliability of Helm chart releases. Automated chart publishing embodies the principle of treating charts as first-class artifacts, subject to rigorous quality gates and repeatable workflows, thereby facilitating smoother operations in cloud-native application delivery.

Chart packaging is the transformation of a Helm chart directory into a compressed chart archive, typically a `.tgz` file. Automating this step ensures that every modification to the chart source triggers the generation of an immutable artifact, ready for deployment or distribution. Within a CI/CD pipeline, packaging can be executed using the Helm CLI command:

```
helm package ./my-chart --destination ./packages
```

Here, the source directory `./my-chart` contains the chart metadata, templates, and configuration files. Automation scripts should manage versioning by updating the `Chart.yaml` semantic version field before packaging, possibly extracting version information from the Git commit history or tags to maintain traceability.

Validation acts as the first level of quality gate, preventing faulty or non-conforming charts from progressing through the pipeline. It typically involves syntactic and semantic checks, adherence to best practices, and prerequisite compatibility validations.

Key validation steps include:

- **Schema Validation**: Ensuring `values.yaml` and `Chart.yaml` conform to defined schemas or conventions.

- **Linting**: Using Helm's built-in linting functionality to catch common errors such as missing templates or incorrect parameter references.

- **Template Rendering**: Rendering templates against provided values to detect rendering failures or incorrect substitution.

- **Security Scanning**: Detecting embedded vulnerabilities or prohibited images within chart container specifications.

A common command to integrate into pipelines is:

```
helm lint ./my-chart
helm template ./my-chart --values=./my-chart/values.yaml
```

Advanced CI/CD systems incorporate external tools such as `ct` (chart-testing), which automate multi-version validations, and may integrate with policy enforcement tools like Open Policy Agent (OPA) to apply organizational standards.

Quality gates enforce thresholds on these validation steps, causing pipeline failures if certain criteria are not met. For example, automated policy checks may prevent charts embedding unapproved container images or lacking required metadata labels from being published.

Upon passing quality gates, packaged charts must be uploaded to a chart repository, which serves as a centralized distribution point. Modern CI/CD pipelines enable automatic uploads to repositories such as:

- **Helm Chart Repositories**: Hosted on object storage services (e.g., AWS S3, Google Cloud Storage) or dedicated chart servers.

- **Artifact Registries**: Systems like GitHub Packages, Harbor, or JFrog Artifactory that support Helm chart format artifacts.

Uploading generally requires authentication setup, secure storage of credentials, and conditional logic to prevent overwriting existing chart versions unless explicitly allowed.

An example upload command using `curl` or a dedicated Helm plugin would look like:

```
curl --data-binary "@./packages/my-chart-1.0.0.tgz" \
    -H "Content-Type: application/octet-stream" \
    -u "username:password" \
    https://charts.example.com/api/charts
```

Alternatively, CI/CD pipeline steps can leverage Helm's push plugin:

```
helm push ./packages/my-chart-1.0.0.tgz oci://registry.example.
    com/charts
```

Using OCI-compliant registries allows uniform management of container images and Helm charts, simplifying security and access control.

A robust pipeline incorporates the aforementioned steps in a strictly ordered fashion with efficient feedback mechanisms:

- Checkout chart source code

- Extract and update chart version metadata

- Run `helm lint` and additional validations

- If validation passes:

    - Package chart artifact with `helm package`

    - Upload chart artifact to repository

    - Tag source control with released version

- Else:

    - Fail the pipeline and report errors

Parallelization of validation and testing tasks can accelerate pipeline throughput. Caching previously validated components and using incremental version updates reduce redundant computation and improve efficiency.

Repeatable releases are guaranteed by immutable chart artifacts tracked to specific source versions. Embedding the source commit SHA or build metadata into chart annotations provides provenance. Reproducible packaging, enabled by consistent environment configurations and dependency management, prevents drift between builds.

Versioning strategies adhering to semantic versioning combined with Git tagging ensure consumers and downstream automation tools can reliably resolve correct chart releases.

Automated chart publishing dramatically reduces manual intervention overhead, enabling development teams to focus on developing features rather than managing release processes. Immediate validation feedback loops facilitate early defect detection, while continuous delivery to artifact repositories enables rapid deployment pipelines downstream.

Furthermore, strict validation and controlled publishing safeguard cluster environments from misconfigurations or unvetted charts, reducing operational incidents and improving overall platform stability.

- Incorporate semantic versioning and automatic version bumping integrated with source control.

- Enforce comprehensive linting, template rendering, and security scanning before packaging.

- Use artifact repositories with fine-grained access controls and immutable storage.

- Embed provenance and build information in chart metadata for traceability.

- Configure pipeline failure conditions on quality gate violations to maintain standards.

- Employ OCI registries for unified management of Helm charts and container images.

- Continuously monitor and optimize pipeline steps for faster releases without compromising quality.

Adhering to these practices transforms Helm chart publishing into a transparent, secure, and efficient process that drives the modernization of cloud-native application delivery pipelines.

6.6. Chart Consumption: Version Pinning, Updates, and Downgrades

Safely consuming software charts in complex deployment environments necessitates rigorous control over dependency versions, systematic strategies for upgrades and downgrades, and mechanisms to precisely reproduce application states. Version pinning establishes a foundation for deterministic deployments by explicitly specifying exact chart versions, thereby avoiding unintended drift caused by transient upstream updates. Upgrading and downgrading charts pose intricate challenges due to potential schema or behavior changes, dependency interactions, and state compatibility considerations. Mastering these processes enables maintainers and operators to manage lifecycle changes confidently, ensuring availability, stability, and traceability.

Version pinning, at its core, is the practice of fixing the dependencies of a Helm chart to a particular version identifier rather than allowing version ranges or floating tags. This guards against semantic versioning mismatches and unpredictable transitive updates. Within a `Chart.yaml` file, dependencies are declared with explicit version strings:

```
dependencies:
  - name: redis
    version: "14.4.0"
    repository: "https://charts.bitnami.com/bitnami"
  - name: cert-manager
    version: "1.11.0"
    repository: "https://charts.jetstack.io"
```

Here, the versions are precise, full versions, typically adhering to SemVer (Semantic Versioning) conventions. This ensures that `helm dependency update` pulls the exact chart archives corresponding to these versions, enabling repeatable builds. Omitting or loosening version constraints to wildcards or ranges (e.g., `>=1.0.0`) risks inconsistent deployments over time. Version pinning also facilitates auditability, as one can reconstruct historical environments based on versioned artifacts.

To evolve an application, upgrades to chart dependencies often become necessary. However, chart upgrades are non-trivial due to the multiple layers of dependencies and Kubernetes resource transformations involved. The Helm ecosystem includes commands to orchestrate upgrades while respecting version control:

```
helm dependency update myapp/
helm upgrade myapp ./myapp-chart
```

A critical prerequisite is to increment the chart version in Chart.yaml and reflect dependency version upgrades only after thorough compatibility verification. Semantic versioning can guide upgrade feasibility: patch and minor version bumps generally promise backward compatibility, whereas major version updates may break API contracts. To avoid cascading failures, operators should verify the changelogs and deprecation notices of all dependency charts before upgrading.

Beyond individual charts, orchestrating upgrades safely requires rehearsed rollback plans. Helm inherently tracks release history, enabling rollbacks to previous application states with:

```
helm rollback myapp 2
```

where 2 signifies the previous revision number. Rollbacks are indispensable for mitigating disruptions when an upgrade introduces incompatibility or failures. However, rollbacks may not always restore mutable application data or stateful sets to prior conditions, especially if changes affect persistent volumes or database schemas. Thus, comprehensive version and state management strategies often need to complement Helm rollbacks with external backup and database migration tools.

Downgrading charts introduces additional complexity, as it often reverses structural or behavioral changes embedded in Kubernetes objects. Helm does not implement downgrade-specific migrations; instead, it applies the older chart manifests as-is. This can lead to resource mismatches or orphaned components if the newer version introduced new resources or fields. To safely perform downgrades, users must:

- Pin dependency versions explicitly before downgrading.

- Carefully examine resource definitions for backward-incompatible changes.

- Execute dry-run deployments (`helm upgrade --install --dry-run`) to preview changes.

- Coordinate database and stateful application downgrades at the application layer.

Failure to perform these steps can cause partial rollbacks or inconsistent cluster states, undermining application reliability.

Reproducing historical application states hinges on access to the exact versions of charts and dependencies originally deployed. Best practices include archiving chart artifacts and dependency packages within internal registries or artifact repositories alongside Helm release metadata. This creates a versioned audit trail enabling redeployment of legacy application states long after upstream charts have evolved or disappeared. Additionally, Helm's `helm get manifest` and `helm get values` commands export the compiled Kubernetes manifests and applied values, facilitating environment reconstruction:

```
helm get manifest myapp > myapp-manifest.yaml
helm get values myapp --output yaml > myapp-values.yaml
```

However, retrieving manifests alone does not guarantee operational equivalence without the pinned chart versions and matching cluster state. Incorporating Infrastructure as Code (IaC) pipelines ensures chart artifacts and values are stored in version control, enabling deterministic continuous delivery. Such reproducibility practices dovetail with version pinning and systematic upgrade/-downgrade procedures to create resilient deployment lifecycles.

Rigorous version pinning prevents unintentional drift and promotes deterministic deployments. Systematic upgrade protocols combined with rollback capabilities mitigate risks during application evolution. Careful downgrade planning is essential due to limited automatic compatibility handling. Finally, maintaining archives and metadata for full reproducibility ensures that deployed application states can be accurately restored or audited. These disciplined consumption practices are vital for stability and flexibility when managing complex Helm-based Kubernetes applications.

Chapter 7

Integrating Helm into CI/CD and GitOps Workflows

Integrating Helm with CI/CD and GitOps isn't just about faster deployments—it's about creating reliable, auditable, and automated infrastructure that scales with your ambitions. This chapter guides you through embedding Helm in the heart of modern delivery pipelines, ensuring every release is consistent, compliant, and observable. Discover how Helm unlocks true continuous delivery, brings order to multi-environment chaos, and empowers teams to move with both speed and safety.

7.1. Helm in Modern Continuous Delivery Pipelines

Helm has become an essential tool for managing Kubernetes applications, offering robust package management capabilities that simplify deployment and lifecycle management. Integrating Helm into continuous integration and continuous delivery (CI/CD) pipelines enhances infrastructure consistency, reduces manual intervention, and accelerates delivery cycles. This integration, however, requires tailored strategies to leverage Helm's features alongside popular CI/CD orchestrators such as GitLab CI, Jenkins, GitHub Actions, and ArgoCD. The following exposition delves into proven approaches, automation essentials, and practical integration points that ensure seamless Helm operation throughout the deployment pipeline.

Automation Fundamentals

Automation within CI/CD pipelines relies heavily on scripting and configuration to execute Helm commands reliably and reproducibly. A foundational practice is to define a clear separation between Helm chart packaging, versioning, linting, and deployment stages, enabling granular control and error isolation. For example, the pipeline typically begins by invoking:

```
helm lint ./charts/myapp
helm package ./charts/myapp --version ${CI_COMMIT_TAG} -d ./
    packaged-charts
```

Linting validates chart structure and metadata, preventing common packaging errors early. Chart packaging produces versioned .tgz artifacts, which can be stored in an artifact repository or Helm chart museum.

Subsequent deployment steps automate Helm-related lifecycle commands such as `helm upgrade`, `helm install`, or `helm rollback`. To maintain idempotency and environment targeting, these commands often incorporate environment-specific values files (e.g., `values-prod.yaml`), managed via templating variables or secret management tools.

Integration Patterns with GitLab CI

GitLab CI's YAML-based pipelines enable declarative, stage-wise orchestration of Helm workflows. A robust pattern involves defining separate jobs for chart linting, packaging, pushing to a Helm repository, and deployment. Helm repositories may be self-hosted or integrated through GitLab's built-in Package Registry.

A typical deployment job illustrates integrating Helm commands in the deployment stage:

```
deploy-prod:
  stage: deploy
  image: alpine/helm:3.8.0
  script:
    - helm repo add myrepo https://helm.example.com/repo
    - helm upgrade --install myapp myrepo/myapp-chart --namespace
      prod -f values-prod.yaml
  environment:
    name: production
    url: https://myapp.example.com
  only:
    - main
```

Here, the Helm Docker image is used as a runner environment, ensuring consistent Helm CLI availability. The command employs --install to accommodate both fresh installations and upgrades, enhancing idempotency in CI/CD executions. To secure cluster access, GitLab CI integrates with Kubernetes through service accounts and secrets mounted as environment variables or configuration files.

Integrating Helm in Jenkins Pipelines

Jenkins pipelines benefit from custom scripted stages or declarative pipeline steps that incorporate Helm commands via shell or container steps. A widely adopted technique involves running Helm commands inside containerized agents, guaranteeing toolchain consistency and reducing dependency-related failures.

An exemplary Jenkins scripted pipeline snippet demonstrates chart deployment:

```
stage('Deploy to Staging') {
    steps {
        container('helm') {
            sh """
```

```
                helm repo add stable https://charts.helm.sh/stable
                helm upgrade --install myapp stable/myapp-chart --
            namespace staging -f values-staging.yaml
                """
            }
        }
}
```

The deployment leverages containerized Helm to abstract the underlying environment. Jenkins credentials plugins can inject Kubernetes configuration and secrets via environment variables or files, ensuring secure cluster interaction. Importantly, pipeline stages separate build, chart validation, and deployment to isolate failures and enable targeted retries.

Utilizing Helm with GitHub Actions

GitHub Actions provides ecosystem-native automation facilitating Helm integration with minimal setup. Reusable actions published by the community offer templated Helm operations, improving maintainability and reducing boilerplate.

A practical GitHub Action workflow for Helm deployment might include:

```
name: Deploy to Kubernetes
on:
  push:
    branches:
      - main

jobs:
  deploy:
    runs-on: ubuntu-latest
    steps:
      - uses: actions/checkout@v3

      - name: Set up Helm
        uses: azure/setup-helm@v1

      - name: Deploy via Helm
        run: |
          helm repo add myrepo https://helm.example.com/repo
          helm upgrade --install myapp myrepo/myapp-chart --
        namespace production -f values-prod.yaml
        env:
```

```
KUBECONFIG: ${{ secrets.KUBECONFIG }}
```

Secrets management through GitHub Secrets (`KUBECONFIG`) facilitates secure cluster credentials injection. The workflow prioritizes simplicity while retaining essential automation-chart retrieval, upgrade/installation, and environment configuration.

ArgoCD and Helm: Declarative Continuous Delivery

ArgoCD embodies declarative GitOps principles, making it a natural complement to Helm. Unlike traditional imperative CI/CD pipelines, ArgoCD continuously monitors Git repositories for Helm chart manifests and applies them to the Kubernetes cluster automatically.

Key integration steps include creating an `Application` manifest referencing a Helm chart repository with appropriate parameters and values override files. An example ArgoCD application using Helm looks like:

```
apiVersion: argoproj.io/v1alpha1
kind: Application
metadata:
  name: myapp
  namespace: argocd
spec:
  project: default
  source:
    repoURL: https://github.com/myorg/myrepo.git
    targetRevision: main
    path: charts/myapp
    helm:
      valueFiles:
        - values-production.yaml
  destination:
    server: https://kubernetes.default.svc
    namespace: production
  syncPolicy:
    automated:
      prune: true
      selfHeal: true
```

ArgoCD automates chart synchronization with cluster state, enabling automatic rollbacks triggered by drift detection or failed health checks. This declarative model minimizes manual intervention by continuously enforcing the desired state defined in Git.

Best Practices and Security Considerations

Effective use of Helm in CI/CD demands adherence to best practices that reduce operational risks. Immutable chart versions should be explicitly referenced to avoid "latest" tags that break reproducibility. Environment values files must be securely managed and never committed in plaintext to version control.

Integration points with RBAC and service accounts should follow the principle of least privilege, limiting Helm's Kubernetes API permissions to only necessary namespaces and resources. Furthermore, secrets injected into pipeline environments should leverage encrypted storage mechanisms native to the CI/CD orchestrator-such as GitLab Vault, Jenkins Credentials, or GitHub Secrets.

Finally, combining Helm with infrastructure-as-code tools (e.g., Terraform, Pulumi) and secret management systems (e.g., HashiCorp Vault) yields robust, secure, and scalable continuous delivery solutions suited for enterprise environments.

Collectively, these strategies and integration patterns reveal that embedding Helm tightly within modern CI/CD frameworks transforms Kubernetes application delivery into a disciplined, repeatable, and scalable process. Each orchestrator offers unique capabilities-leveraged correctly-to unlock the full benefits of Helm's package-driven deployment model.

7.2. GitOps Paradigms and Helm Integration

GitOps is an operational framework that leverages Git repositories as the single source of truth for declarative infrastructure and application management. At its core, GitOps relies on the principle that the entire desired state of a system is version-controlled, auditable, and subject to standard software development workflows. This approach enables pull-based infrastructure management, where automated agents continuously reconcile the live system state against the state declared within Git. Any detected divergence triggers corrective actions, resulting in drift-free and self-healing environments.

The central tenet of GitOps is the declarative specification of the intended state. Unlike imperative approaches, where operators manually execute procedural commands to manipulate infrastructure, declarative models express *what* the system should look like rather than *how* to achieve it. This separation enhances reproducibility and reliability because human operators no longer depend on manual steps prone to error or inconsistency. Instead, the application of changes is exclusively driven by transitioning from one Git commit to another, and the operational platform applies those changes continuously and deterministically.

Helm, as a package manager for Kubernetes, facilitates encapsulating complex Kubernetes manifests into reusable, parameterized charts. Helm charts, representing collections of YAML templates augmented with logic and configuration parameters, are ideal artifacts for GitOps workflows. They abstract the procedural complexity embedded in Kubernetes YAML files and provide a clean interface for application configuration and lifecycle management. When integrated into a GitOps toolchain, Helm charts become first-class citizens, positioning packaging, deployment, and upgrade automation alongside infrastructure declarations.

A primary challenge GitOps addresses is state drift, where the actual cluster configuration departs from the intended specification, possibly due to manual ad-hoc changes, failures during deployments, or external system effects. Helm charts, when managed declaratively within Git repositories and deployed via GitOps agents (such as Argo CD or Flux), ensure synchronization by monitoring Helm release states. These tools invoke Helm as a reconciliation engine that applies the chart's rendered manifests and monitors Helm-specific metadata, such as release version and history. The continuous presence of the Helm chart in Git and its correlation with the cluster state guarantees automatic remediation in case of drift-downtime or configuration inconsistencies are minimized.

Consider the following conceptual model of Helm integration within a GitOps-driven environment. The Git repository contains a structured layout:

- A directory storing Helm charts representing individual applications or microservices.

- Environment-specific overlays consisting of values files that parameterize Helm charts to fit the unique requirements of staging, production, or development.

- Automation scripts or manifests to bootstrap GitOps tools and configure reconciliation intervals.

The GitOps agent monitors this repository and, upon detecting new commits, follows these steps:

1. Fetch and validate the updated Helm chart contents and values.

2. Render the Helm templates locally to produce the Kubernetes manifests.

3. Perform a three-way diff between the live cluster state, the last applied manifest, and the freshly rendered manifests.

4. Execute the Helm upgrade, install, or rollback commands as required, ensuring the cluster matches the desired configuration.

This process is inherently idempotent; failed deployments can be retried without unintended side effects, and rollback is straightforward by reverting the Git commit.

An example Helm-based GitOps configuration could be represented through the following minimal manifest stored under `environments/prod/values.yaml`:

```
replicaCount: 3
image:
  repository: myorg/myapp
  tag: v1.2.0
service:
  type: LoadBalancer
  port: 80
```

Together with the Helm chart stored in `charts/myapp/`, this values file defines the precise application deployment for the production environment.

GitOps platforms augment Helm operations by exposing health and status metrics of Helm releases, adding visibility to deployment pipelines. They reconcile not only application manifests but also cluster infrastructure components, enabling operators to manage complex stacks with consistent tooling. Helm's templating flexibility supports modular charts, which can be integrated hierarchically or with dependencies, and GitOps pipelines further enforce semantic versioning of charts, ensuring orderly upgrades and minimizing disruption.

In scenarios demanding multicluster or multi-tenant deployments, GitOps coupled with Helm charts fosters scalability and governance. By controlling chart versions and environment-specific overrides in a centralized Git repository, teams achieve compliance and traceability. Furthermore, integrating GitOps with Helm reduces cognitive load, as deployment changes are fully codified and peer-reviewed through Git pull requests, maintaining rigorous change control.

Security considerations benefit from this approach as well. Since

Helm charts and values files are stored in Git repositories, automated security scans, policy enforcements, and secrets management can be embedded within the CI/CD pipeline. GitOps agents can be configured to reject non-compliant manifests prior to deployment, enforcing best practices throughout the lifecycle.

In essence, the symbiotic relationship between GitOps paradigms and Helm empowers organizations to adopt declarative, version-driven infrastructure workflows, particularly suited for cloud-native Kubernetes environments. Here, Helm charts serve not only as deployment artifacts but as integral components of a robust, automated system that guarantees drift-free, self-healing clusters with full traceability and reproducibility.

7.3. Automating Quality Gates and Policy Enforcement

Ensuring robustness and compliance in continuous delivery pipelines demands the integration of automated quality gates and policy enforcement mechanisms. By embedding these controls early in the deployment lifecycle, organizations can substantially reduce the risk of introducing defects, misconfigurations, or security vulnerabilities into production environments. This section elucidates the practical incorporation of Helm linting, template validation, and policy-as-code frameworks as fundamental components to enforce quality and security standards in Kubernetes application delivery.

Helm, as the de facto package manager for Kubernetes, facilitates templated application manifest management. Yet, its templating nature introduces risks of errors, such as missing values or invalid syntax, which can only be detected at runtime if left unverified. Helm linting serves as an initial static analysis tool that inspects charts for common issues, adherence to best practices, and consistency. Executing the `helm lint` command provides immediate feedback by flagging deprecated API usage, incorrect chart meta-data, or syntactic anomalies in templates. Integrating this step at the onset of the pipeline automates detection of low-hanging faults before manifest rendering.

However, linting alone is insufficient to guarantee that generated Kubernetes manifests are both syntactically sound and semantically valid in the target cluster context. To complement linting, template validation processes should be employed. This involves rendering Helm charts into Kubernetes manifests using the `helm template` command, thereby expanding all charts and values into pure YAML resources. These manifests can then be validated using Kubernetes API schema validation tools such as `kubectl apply --dry-run=server` or third-party validators. Detection of schema violations, unresolved variables, or invalid field values at this phase acts as a critical gate, preventing misconfigured resources from progressing further in the pipeline.

The combination of linting and template validation addresses structural and syntactic correctness; nonetheless, enforcement of organizational policies and security controls requires a programmable, extensible framework. Policy-as-code frameworks underpin this objective by codifying policies as declarative rules evaluated against the application manifests. Frameworks such as Open Policy Agent (OPA) and its Kubernetes-specific extension Gatekeeper provide expressive languages (e.g., Rego) to author constraints that define permitted or forbidden resource configurations. These policies can capture complex compliance requirements including mandatory labels, resource quota limitations, security context mandates, or disallowed container images.

Integrating policy evaluation as an automated quality gate creates a checkpoint that decisively enforces governance before deployment. For example, a policy may specify that all Pods enforce non-root user execution or that specific namespaces must not expose services of type `LoadBalancer`. Deploying Gatekeeper in a validation webhook mode enables real-time admission control in live clusters; however, preemptive policy checks against rendered manifests in a CI/CD pipeline stage further prevent forbidden changes from reaching cluster admission. This dual-stage enforcement ensures comprehensive coverage.

Typical pipeline implementation involves sequencing these steps:

- Execute `helm lint` on the chart to detect syntax and metadata issues.

- Generate Kubernetes manifests via `helm template` with appropriate values.

- Validate manifests with `kubectl apply --dry-run=server` or equivalent validation tools.

- Evaluate rendered manifests against policy-as-code rules using OPA or Gatekeeper tools.

- If any step fails, halt the pipeline and return detailed diagnostics to developers.

- Otherwise, proceed to artifact packaging and deployment stages.

Automation of these gates generates immediate and actionable insights for development and operations teams, reducing the mean time to detection of faults and decreasing manual review overhead. Moreover, the declarative nature of policy-as-code frameworks facilitates version control, auditability, and evolution of policies consistent with shifting security and compliance landscapes.

Effective integration requires attention to several technical considerations. Helm chart designers must ensure completeness and correctness of `values.yaml` files; iterative linting and validation uncover common pitfalls such as missing required values or un-supported constructs. Pipeline tooling should support parallel execution of linting and validation stages to optimize feedback time. Policy coders must craft rules with precision to avoid false positives that hinder delivery velocity, balancing security strictness with operational practicality.

The output from these automated gates should include rich diagnostics. For example, the following helm lint invocation and output illustrate typical feedback:

```
$ helm lint my-chart
==> Linting my-chart
[INFO] Chart.yaml: icon is recommended

1 chart(s) linted, 0 chart(s) failed
```

Similarly, template validation with server-side dry-run produces feedback in a Kubernetes-native format:

```
$ kubectl apply -f rendered.yaml --dry-run=server
Error from server (Invalid): error when creating "rendered.yaml":
PodSecurityContext must specify runAsNonRoot when securityContext is set
```

Finally, policy evaluation results with OPA or Gatekeeper articulate violations explicitly, for example:

```
violation: Pod runs as root user
resource: Pod/my-application-abc123
message: All containers must run as non-root for compliance
```

Together, these automated quality gates and policy enforcements create a resilient gatekeeper combination ensuring that only manifests meeting syntactic, semantic, and organizational standards advance through continuous delivery pipelines. This systematic approach strengthens confidence in Kubernetes application security and operational correctness well before reaching live deployments.

7.4. Automated Promotion and Environment Management

In complex Kubernetes deployment pipelines, managing application promotion through multiple environments—development, staging, and production—necessitates a systematic approach that ensures consistency, repeatability, and safety. Helm, as a package manager for Kubernetes, offers powerful primitives to automate and streamline this multi-stage deployment flow, while addressing environment-specific configurations and rollback strategies. This section dissects key mechanisms and best practices to achieve this automation.

At the heart of automated promotion lies the concept of *versioned Helm charts* and *parameterized values*. Each deployment artifact corresponds to a Helm chart version encapsulating a specific application release. Lifecycle promotion involves incrementally upgrading target environments using appropriate chart versions, controlled through continuous integration and deployment (CI/CD) pipelines. This practice prevents configuration drift and promotes traceability.

Environment-Specific Overrides

Kubernetes environments invariably differ in resource limits, ingress rules, secrets, monitoring integrations, and other parameters. Helm's separation of chart templates and values files facilitates clean environment-specific overrides without duplicating manifest code. A canonical approach involves maintaining a base chart with default values coupled with environment-specific values files:

```
helm upgrade --install myapp ./myapp-chart \
  --namespace development --values values-dev.yaml
helm upgrade --install myapp ./myapp-chart \
  --namespace staging --values values-staging.yaml
helm upgrade --install myapp ./myapp-chart \
  --namespace production --values values-production.yaml
```

Each values file tailors configurations such as replica counts, re-source requests, or feature flags to the operational characteristics and policies of that environment. This method enforces consistency by versioning these values files in the same repository as the Helm chart itself.

Automated Promotion Using CI/CD

A robust CI/CD workflow connects Helm chart packaging, testing, and deployment stages, automating the promotion chain. After committing application code and Helm charts, pipelines run static validation, unit tests, and integration tests on ephemeral Kubernetes clusters (e.g., using KinD or Minikube). Upon success, the chart is packaged and pushed to a Helm chart repository with semantic versioning, e.g., using ChartMuseum or integrated cloud registries.

Promotion across environments is controlled by pipeline stages, each referencing specific chart versions and values overrides. The promotion logic can be scripted via Helm CLI calls, templated in pipeline definitions, or handled by dedicated GitOps tools:

```
helm upgrade --install myapp ./myapp-chart \
  --namespace staging --values values-staging.yaml \
  --version 1.2.0

helm upgrade --install myapp ./myapp-chart \
  --namespace production --values values-production.yaml \
  --version 1.2.0
```

Here, the same application version (1.2.0) is successively deployed to staging and then production, thereby maintaining synchronization between these environments. The use of exact version numbers avoids ambiguity and prevents accidental promotion of untested or incompatible releases.

Robust Rollback Strategies

Despite thorough testing, operational environments may require rapid rollbacks when failures or regressions occur post-deployment. Helm's intrinsic support for release history and rollback simplifies recovery. Each Helm upgrade creates a new release revision, indexed chronologically. Invoking:

```
helm rollback myapp <revision>
```

restores the cluster state to a previous known good configuration, reverting all Kubernetes resources controlled by that release. Maintaining a clear release history and configuring Helm with an appropriate maximum release count (via `--history-max`) ensures rollback capability without excessive state retention.

Atomic upgrades with the `--atomic` flag further enhance safety by attempting full rollbacks automatically if a deployment fails:

```
helm upgrade --install myapp ./myapp-chart \
  --namespace production --values values-production.yaml \
  --atomic
```

If errors occur during the upgrade, Helm reverts changes to the prior release state, thus preventing partial or inconsistent deployments.

Managing Secrets and Sensitive Data Across Environments

A consistent promoting workflow must carefully handle secrets and sensitive configurations, which vary per environment and require secure management. Helm does not natively encrypt secrets; hence, integration with external secret management tools or Kubernetes native constructs is essential. One established pattern is to refrain from embedding secrets directly in Helm values files. Instead, Helm templates reference Kubernetes `Secret` objects pre-created or synchronized from vaults such as HashiCorp Vault, AWS Secrets Manager, or Sealed Secrets.

An example in Helm templates might be:

```
env:
  - name: DB_PASSWORD
    valueFrom:
      secretKeyRef:
```

```
    name: db-secret
    key: password
```

This abstraction enables environment-specific secret provisioning independent of Helm configuration parameters, preserving promotion flexibility while maintaining security boundaries.

Idempotency and Declarative Consistency

For promotion automation to be reliable, Helm deployments must be idempotent, ensuring that repeated executions with identical inputs produce stable cluster states. This principle reduces deployment flakiness and mitigates side effects. Using deterministic values files and explicit chart versioning contributes to idempotency. Additionally, extensive use of Helm template functions for conditional resource definitions and environment variables fine-tunes deployments without introducing divergence.

Example Multi-Stage Promotion Pipeline

Consider a simplified promotion sequence integrated in Jenkins or GitHub Actions:

```
Build application container image and push to registry with tag
    vX.Y.Z
Package Helm chart with updated app image tag and version X.Y.Z
Deploy to development cluster:
  helm upgrade --install myapp ./chart --namespace dev --values
    values-dev.yaml --version X.Y.Z
Run integration and acceptance tests against development
    environment
if tests pass:
  Promote to staging:
    helm upgrade --install myapp ./chart --namespace staging --
    values values-staging.yaml --version X.Y.Z
  Run staging validation and manual sign-off
  if validated:
    Promote to production:
      helm upgrade --install myapp ./chart --namespace production
      --values values-production.yaml --version X.Y.Z --atomic
  else:
    Rollback staging release if necessary
else:
  Abort promotion, fix issues, and redeploy development
```

This linear flow enforces control gates and aligns deployments across environments while automating promotion tasks with explicit semantic versioning and environment-specific values segregation.

Automated promotion and environment management using Helm reduces manual toil and error, improves auditability, and accelerates delivery cycles. Effective use of version control, environment-specific overrides, atomic upgrades, and controlled rollbacks are indispensable practices. Combined with secure secret handling and idempotent deployments, they comprise a comprehensive framework to govern high-velocity Kubernetes application rollouts across fluctuating operational landscapes.

7.5. Secrets, Keys, and Access Control in CI/CD

The effective management of secrets and cryptographic keys, alongside rigorous access control, constitutes a fundamental pillar for securing modern Continuous Integration and Continuous Deployment (CI/CD) pipelines. The inherently automated and ephemeral nature of CI/CD workflows introduces distinct challenges in safeguarding credentials while maintaining operational agility. This section delves into the orchestration of ephemeral credentials, enforcement of least-privilege access, and stringent repository and cluster access controls to mitigate risks stemming from credential leakage and unauthorized access within automated systems.

Ephemeral Credentials: Reducing Exposure and Impact

Long-lived static credentials represent a significant attack surface in automated pipelines. Exfiltration or accidental leakage of such secrets can result in unauthorized access to infrastructure and services, potentially leading to full-scale compromise. To minimize this risk, CI/CD systems increasingly employ ephemeral credentials-a strategy where secrets and keys exist only for the brief duration required by a pipeline task or job.

Ephemeral credentials are typically provisioned dynamically through integrations with secrets management platforms or cloud identity services. For example, a pipeline may request short-lived OAuth tokens, IAM roles, or session-based API keys via a trusted broker just prior to deployment or testing. These credentials automatically expire, significantly reducing the window of opportunity for malicious actors.

An example is the use of HashiCorp Vault's dynamic secrets engine:

```
vault read database/creds/ci-role
```

This command dynamically generates a database credential with a short time-to-live (TTL), scoped specifically to the CI job's requirements. Once the TTL lapses or the workflow completes, the secret is revoked, nullifying access. This dynamic generation and revocation paradigm is essential for minimizing credential sprawl across ephemeral pipeline environments.

Tightly Controlled Repository and Cluster Access

Access controls must be strictly enforced both at the source code repository level and on deployment clusters. Repositories often hold secrets in configuration files or environment variables unless managed conscientiously, creating a vector for sensitive information exposure. Strict policies should be implemented to scan for accidental secret injection and enforce encryption-at-rest and in-transit.

Role-Based Access Control (RBAC) mechanisms within source control systems and container orchestration platforms like Kubernetes are critical to enforce least-privilege policies. Assigning minimal roles to CI/CD service accounts and scheduled workflows prevents unauthorized operations, such as code merges or cluster modifications beyond their scope.

In Kubernetes, for example, access can be restricted by defining ServiceAccounts with precise Role and RoleBinding constructs:

```
apiVersion: rbac.authorization.k8s.io/v1
kind: Role
metadata:
  namespace: production
  name: deployer
rules:
- apiGroups: ["apps"]
  resources: ["deployments"]
  verbs: ["get", "update", "patch"]
---
apiVersion: v1
kind: ServiceAccount
metadata:
  name: ci-cd-deployer
  namespace: production
---
apiVersion: rbac.authorization.k8s.io/v1
kind: RoleBinding
metadata:
  name: deployer-binding
  namespace: production
subjects:
- kind: ServiceAccount
  name: ci-cd-deployer
  namespace: production
roleRef:
  kind: Role
  name: deployer
  apiGroup: rbac.authorization.k8s.io
```

This example tightly restricts the deployment capabilities of a CI/CD pipeline component, allowing only specific updates on deployment resources, ensuring no overreach occurs in the Kubernetes cluster.

Principle of Least Privilege for Automated Systems

The automation inherent to CI/CD pipelines necessitates the principle of least privilege to reduce the blast radius of a compromised component or pipeline. Least privilege mandates that every component, service account, and pipeline step have exactly the permissions necessary and nothing more.

Applying least privilege begins with scoping credentials to the minimum set of resources and actions. For instance, API tokens used during build phases should not carry permissions for deployment or cluster administration. Conversely, deployment credentials should not allow code repository access or secret management beyond what is required for rollout.

Credential segmentation also enables granular audit trails and simplifies incident response. When credentials are individual and minimal, identifying the source of a security event is more straightforward, and revoking or rotating affected keys can be performed without wide collateral disruption.

Secure Storage and Injection of Secrets

Secrets should never be hardcoded, embedded in source code, or committed to version control systems. Instead, secrets are stored in dedicated secret management systems that provide encryption, access control, audit logging, and automatic rotation capabilities. Integration with CI/CD pipelines ensures secrets are injected into runtime environments only when needed, preserving confidentiality.

Secure secret injection methods typically leverage environment variables, mounted volumes, or API calls within build agents and runners, often via transient sidecar containers or ephemeral credential fetch commands. These injection methods keep secrets out of static configuration files and minimize exposure to unintended processes.

Auditing, Monitoring, and Automated Remediation

An effective secret and key management strategy includes continuous auditing and monitoring of secret access patterns and usage anomalies. Automated alerts on irregular access and transaction patterns help detect potential compromise early. Combining audit logs from secrets managers, version control systems, and cluster access logs provides a comprehensive security posture.

Where possible, automated remediations such as immediate credential revocation, pipeline job cancellations, or container rollbacks further reduce risk from leaked or abused secrets. Proactive observability ensures that the pipeline infrastructure remains resilient against evolving threat vectors targeting secret and key management vulnerabilities.

Integration Best Practices for Secrets and Access Control

To operationalize these principles, organizations adopt several best practices:

- Use identity-based access controls: employ cloud or federation identities over static secrets where available, leveraging short-lived tokens.

- Enforce multi-factor authentication (MFA): particularly for privileged users and system accounts interacting with secret stores.

- Segregate environments: separate dev, staging, and production secrets and access controls to prevent lateral movement.

- Review and rotate credentials: implement periodic and event-driven key rotation policies to limit stale credentials.

- Automate secret scanning: integrate secret scanning tools into commit and merge workflows to detect accidental disclosures.

- Document and version control access policies: maintain transparent policies to facilitate governance and compliance.

The intertwining of secret lifecycle management, fine-grained access control, and automation-hardening measures forms the cornerstone of secure CI/CD pipelines. These strategies ensure that the accelerating velocity and scale of software delivery do not come at the cost of increased attack surface or operational risk.

7.6. Monitoring and Observability Integration

Helm charts traditionally facilitate streamlined application deployment and lifecycle management in Kubernetes environments. To achieve comprehensive operational visibility, integrating telemetry into Helm-managed applications is a critical evolution that enables real-time insight and rapid troubleshooting throughout the delivery pipeline. Telemetry data-encompassing metrics, logs, and traces-forms the backbone of effective observability. This section details practical strategies for embedding telemetry export mechanisms directly into your Helm charts, focusing on modularity, scalability, and maintainability.

Embedding Prometheus metrics into your Helm charts should adopt the `ServiceMonitor` custom resource definitions (CRDs) provided by the `prometheus-operator`, ensuring seamless discovery and scraping of application endpoints.

A typical Helm values snippet enabling Prometheus metrics might look like:

```
metrics:
  enabled: true
  port: 9100
  path: /metrics
```

In the template definitions, ensure that a container port and readiness probe correspond to the metrics endpoint:

```
ports:
  - name: metrics
    containerPort: {{ .Values.metrics.port }}
    protocol: TCP

readinessProbe:
  httpGet:
    path: {{ .Values.metrics.path }}
    port: metrics
```

```
initialDelaySeconds: 10
periodSeconds: 10
```

For the `ServiceMonitor`, the Helm template might include:

```
apiVersion: monitoring.coreos.com/v1
kind: ServiceMonitor
metadata:
  name: {{ include "myapp.fullname" . }}-metrics
  labels:
    release: {{ .Release.Name }}
spec:
  selector:
    matchLabels:
      app: {{ include "myapp.name" . }}
  endpoints:
  - port: metrics
    path: {{ .Values.metrics.path }}
    interval: 15s
```

This declarative setup allows the Prometheus operator to automatically discover and scrape the application's metrics endpoints without manual intervention. Where Prometheus is not available, consider exposing the metrics endpoint to external monitoring platforms using appropriate service types and ingress configurations.

Application logs provide unstructured but rich context for diagnosing issues, especially when combined with metrics and traces. Integration of logging frameworks into a Helm chart requires attention to log format consistency and the log pipeline architecture.

Within Kubernetes, a common pattern involves writing application logs to standard output (stdout) in structured JSON format. This allows the cluster-level log collector (such as Fluentd, Fluent Bit, or Logstash) to ingest logs consistently, regardless of application name or version.

Configure your container with environment variables that enable structured logging as demonstrated below:

```
env:
  - name: LOG_LEVEL
    value: "info"
  - name: LOG_FORMAT
    value: "json"
```

To facilitate metadata enrichment, include Kubernetes downward API annotations in your pod spec for contextual labels:

```
metadata:
  labels:
    app: {{ include "myapp.name" . }}
    release: {{ .Release.Name }}
  annotations:
    logging.kubernetes.io/pod: "{{ .Release.Name }}-{{ .Chart.
    Name }}"
```

Log aggregation is normally handled by cluster-level DaemonSets that tail container logs and forward data to a centralized system like Elasticsearch or Loki. Ensuring consistent log format and embedding labels via annotations allows filtered querying and correlation across services.

Tracing enriches observability by capturing causal execution paths through distributed systems. OpenTelemetry has unified tracing instrumentation and exporter standards, providing language-agnostic SDKs and exporters.

To integrate tracing in Helm charts, you must:

- Enable tracing configuration in application deployment.

- Deploy or reference a tracing backend, such as Jaeger or Zipkin.

- Configure exporters to transmit trace data to the backend.

Helm values can include:

```
tracing:
  enabled: true
  serviceName: myapp
  exporter:
    jaeger:
      endpoint: http://jaeger-collector.my-namespace.svc.cluster.
      local:14268/api/traces
```

Your deployment template injects necessary environment variables and sidecar containers if needed:

```
env:
  - name: OTEL_SERVICE_NAME
    value: {{ .Values.tracing.serviceName }}
  - name: OTEL_EXPORTER_JAEGER_ENDPOINT
    value: {{ .Values.tracing.exporter.jaeger.endpoint }}
```

If using OpenTelemetry Collector as a central agent, deploy it alongside the application pods or at a cluster level, and configure your application to send traces to the collector's endpoint. This decouples sampling and backend complexity from the application.

The integration strategy must consider security, resource utilization, and upgrade compatibility:

- **Security:** Configure Role-Based Access Control (RBAC) correctly for metrics scraping and log access. Use secure TLS endpoints where possible and avoid exposing telemetry endpoints to untrusted networks.

- **Resource Management:** Instrumentation adds overhead. Employ resource requests and limits in Helm charts to guarantee predictable runtime behavior for telemetry components.

- **Configuration Management:** Use Helm's templating capabilities to propagate default instrumentation settings while allowing overrides via values files, enabling environment-specific tuning without code changes.

The ultimate goal of telemetry integration into Helm charts is to close the feedback loop in the delivery pipeline. By combining metrics, logs, and traces:

- **Metrics** enable early anomaly detection through continuous monitoring and alerting.

- **Logs** provide granular diagnostic details essential for root cause analysis.

- **Traces** reveal request flows and service dependencies, aiding performance optimization and error tracing.

Consider a scenario in which application latency spikes; the metrics alert furnishes the initial indication. Investigating correlated traces shows bottlenecks in downstream services, while logs uncover error patterns or misconfigurations. This integrated workflow accelerates mean time to resolution (MTTR) and maintains system reliability.

In practice, equip your Helm charts with smart defaults for telemetry exporters and dashboards. Use automated tests during chart validation to assert that telemetry endpoints respond as expected, ensuring consistent observability across deployment environments.

The design and deployment of observability components alongside your Helm-managed applications establish the foundation for mature DevOps practices, empowering teams to deliver with confidence and agility.

Chapter 8

Security and Compliance in Helm Deployments

As organizations entrust increasingly sensitive workloads to Kubernetes, security and compliance become essential—not optional—ingredients in every Helm chart deployment. This chapter demystifies the practices and policies that empower you to safeguard supply chains, enforce governance, and respond swiftly to threats. Gain actionable strategies for risk mitigation, structured review, and ongoing compliance, making security an organic part of every Helm-powered workflow.

8.1. Securing Helm Operations

The security of Kubernetes deployments fundamentally extends to the management tooling that interacts with the cluster. Helm, as the predominant package manager for Kubernetes, necessitates rigorous hardening measures to safeguard operational integrity and prevent unauthorized cluster modifications. This begins with a comprehensive application of Role-Based Access Control (RBAC), continues through secure repository management, and concludes with enforcing strict privilege controls to ensure that only authenticated and authorized entities can perform impactful changes.

Role-Based Access Control (RBAC) Configuration

RBAC is a critical security mechanism that restricts user access to Kubernetes resources based on defined roles and permissions. Helm's reliance on Kubernetes API operations mandates careful RBAC policy definitions tailored to the Helm service accounts and operators. To implement a secure RBAC configuration for Helm, three considerations are paramount:

1. **Limiting Helm's scope of access to namespaces:** Grants should be namespace-specific whenever feasible. Helm service accounts should only be given permissions within the namespaces where releases are deployed, rather than cluster-wide privileges.

2. **Minimal requisite permissions:** The principle of least privilege should guide the allowance of resource verbs (e.g., get, list, watch, create, update, and delete). Helm needs access primarily to ConfigMaps and Secrets (used for storing release data), and to resources defined by charts, but excessive privileges on unforeseen resources significantly widen the attack surface.

3. **Distinct service accounts for CI/CD pipelines and human operators:** Separation enables granular auditability and restricts automation systems and users to their assigned permissions.

An exemplary RBAC Role definition binding a Helm service account to namespace-limited permissions might appear as follows:

```
apiVersion: rbac.authorization.k8s.io/v1
kind: Role
metadata:
  namespace: production
  name: helm-user
rules:
- apiGroups: [""]
  resources: ["configmaps", "secrets"]
  verbs: ["get", "list", "watch", "create", "update", "delete"]
- apiGroups: ["apps", "batch", "extensions"]
  resources: ["deployments", "statefulsets", "jobs", "daemonsets
    "]
  verbs: ["get", "list", "watch", "create", "update", "delete"]
```

This role should be bound to the appropriate Helm service account via a RoleBinding:

```
apiVersion: rbac.authorization.k8s.io/v1
kind: RoleBinding
metadata:
  name: helm-user-binding
  namespace: production
subjects:
- kind: ServiceAccount
  name: helm-sa
  namespace: production
roleRef:
  kind: Role
  name: helm-user
  apiGroup: rbac.authorization.k8s.io
```

Securing Helm Repository Management

Helm repositories serve as the source of charts-templates and definitions that instantiate complex Kubernetes applications. Ensuring the authenticity and integrity of these charts is as critical as controlling access to cluster resources. Several strategies achieve effective repository security:

- **TLS-enforced communication and trusted repositories:** Always configure Helm to communicate with repositories over HTTPS with validated certificates. This prevents tampering and man-in-the-middle attacks during chart downloads.

- **Authenticated repository access:** For private repositories, apply strict authentication protocols via tokens, user-
  name/password, or other API keys. Avoid embedding credentials in Helm command lines or manifests; prefer environment variables or Kubernetes secrets.

- **Chart provenance verification:** Utilize Helm's built-in
  capability for verifying provenance files (.prov), which provide cryptographic signatures of charts. These signatures validate the source and integrity of charts before installation.

- **Repository replication and mirroring:** For enterprise
  scenarios, establish internal Helm chart registries or mirrors
  behind firewall boundaries to limit external exposure and increase control over chart distribution.

A typical secure repository addition command using TLS and authentication tokens is illustrated below:

```
helm repo add secure-repo https://charts.securecorp.com \
  --username secureuser --password <token_or_password>
```

Before installation, verify the provenance file as:

```
helm verify mychart-1.2.3.tgz
```

Provenance verification ensures the chart has not been modified
since signing and originates from a trusted authority.

Strict Privilege Controls and Best Practices

Beyond RBAC and repository security, additional controls enhance
the hardened posture of Helm operations:

1. **Use of the `--atomic` flag in Helm installs/updates:**
   This flag automates rollback on failed deployments, preventing partial or inconsistent states that could expose vulnerabilities or operational instability.

2. **Restrict Helm tiller access where applicable:**

Although Helm 3 removed the server-side Tiller component, legacy Helm 2 installations still require tight RBAC rules explicitly denying user groups unauthorized Tiller access.

3. **Audit logging and monitoring:** Enable Kubernetes audit logs focused on RBAC decision events and resource accesses initiated by Helm service accounts. These logs provide traceability for security investigations and compliance reporting.

4. **Limiting Helm operations in CI/CD pipelines:** Containers running Helm commands in automated pipelines should run with the least privileges possible and in isolated runtime contexts. Where feasible, the pipelines should leverage short-lived tokens dynamically provisioned and revoked.

5. **Avoid overprivileged ClusterRole bindings:** Abstain from granting Helm a `cluster-admin` role, which provides excessive and unrestricted access to cluster-wide resources. Custom ClusterRoles must be narrowly scoped based on operational requirements.

6. **Secret management hygiene:** Helm stores release metadata in Kubernetes `Secrets` or `ConfigMaps`. Employ encryption-at-rest mechanisms for etcd, restrict access to these Kubernetes secrets, and periodically review the content for sensitive information leakage.

Helm Security Policy Example

Consider a final example demonstrating a tightly scoped Cluster-Role augmenting namespace roles while explicitly disallowing hazardous permissions:

```
apiVersion: rbac.authorization.k8s.io/v1
kind: ClusterRole
metadata:
  name: helm-limited-clusterrole
rules:
- apiGroups: [""]
  resources: ["configmaps", "secrets"]
  verbs: ["get", "list", "watch", "create", "update", "delete"]
```

```
- apiGroups: ["apps"]
  resources: ["deployments", "statefulsets", "daemonsets"]
  verbs: ["get", "list", "watch", "create", "update", "delete"]
- apiGroups: ["batch"]
  resources: ["jobs"]
  verbs: ["get", "list", "watch", "create", "update", "delete"]
# Explicitly exclude resources like nodes, persistentvolumes, and
      clusterroles
```

This fine-grained ClusterRole can be bound to Helm service accounts that manage multi-namespace deployments without granting cluster-wide superuser powers.

Securing Helm operations demands attentiveness to both Kubernetes-native access control and Helm-specific operational modes. Through disciplined RBAC configurations, stringent management of chart repositories, and vigilant privilege controls, organizations can significantly reduce their risk of cluster compromise via Helm. The integration of Helm's authentication and signature verification mechanisms ensures that only vetted and authorized actors modify cluster state, maintaining operational stability and protecting critical workloads.

8.2. Vulnerability Management in Dependencies

Effective vulnerability management in dependencies is critical for maintaining the security posture of modern software deployments, particularly those leveraging package charts and containerized environments. Dependencies-including Helm charts and container images-often introduce external code risks that must be rigorously assessed, tracked, and mitigated to prevent exploitation. This section details systematic approaches and tools for vulnerability management, focusing on scanning methodologies, continuous tracking, and structured update workflows.

The initial step in managing vulnerabilities lies in thorough assessment. This involves automated identification of known security flaws within the components incorporated in charts and container images. For Helm charts, vulnerabilities can arise from the libraries and subcharts used, as well as from the base images of containers specified within the deployment manifests.

Container image vulnerability assessment typically relies on scanning tools that analyze operating system packages, language runtime dependencies, and installed software layers. Prominent scanners such as `Trivy`, `Clair`, and `Anchore` inspect image layers for CVEs (Common Vulnerabilities and Exposures), drawing from databases like the National Vulnerability Database (NVD) and vendor advisories.

For Helm charts, tools like `chart-testing` combined with static analysis utilities can detect insecure configurations or outdated dependencies. Additionally, integrating software composition analysis (SCA) tools enables identification of vulnerable libraries declared in chart dependencies or container build specifications.

A robust tracking system forms the backbone of managing vulnerability lifecycles in dependencies. It entails continuous monitoring for newly disclosed vulnerabilities relevant to the software supply chain components used in production.

Centralized vulnerability databases must be synchronized frequently to include the latest CVE information. Automated pipelines can facilitate this synchronization and correlate findings with the versions of dependencies currently deployed.

The aggregation of vulnerability data is often orchestrated through dashboard platforms that provide visibility into severity, exploitability, and remediation status. Maintaining metadata about component versions, scan timestamps, and patch histories ensures accurate impact analysis.

An example workflow involves integrating Continuous Integration/Continuous Deployment (CI/CD) pipelines with scanning tools that generate vulnerability reports upon each build or release. Alerts triggered by discovery of critical vulnerabilities ensure rapid stakeholder response, prioritizing fixes based on business risk.

Patching vulnerable dependencies demands a disciplined, repeatable update workflow that minimizes disruption while ensuring security integrity. The patching process includes identification of remediations, validation, deployment, and verification steps.

Identification of Remediations: Once vulnerabilities are detected and assessed, the next task is to locate remediation patches or updated package versions. For container images, this typically involves upgrading the base image tags and the packages installed via package managers. For Helm charts, updated chart versions or fixed subcharts are procured from trusted repositories.

Validation: Before deploying patched dependencies, validation is critical to ensure compatibility and function correctness. Automated tests, including unit, integration, and security tests, verify that updates do not introduce regressions or new vulnerabilities.

Deployment: Patch deployment workflows often leverage CI/CD automation to rebuild container images and redeploy Helm charts with updated dependency versions. The deployment can utilize blue/green or canary strategies to reduce risk and provide rollback capabilities.

Verification: Post-deployment, rescanning is performed to confirm that vulnerabilities have been effectively remediated. Runtime verification can include behavioral monitoring and intrusion detection to detect any anomalous activity or exploitation attempts.

A typical workflow to integrate vulnerability scanning into the development lifecycle uses `Trivy`, a versatile and fast container image scanner, embedded into the CI pipeline as follows:

```
# Scan the Docker image for vulnerabilities
```

```
trivy image --severity HIGH,CRITICAL myrepo/myimage:latest >
    vulns_report.txt

# Check if vulnerabilities were found
if grep -q "CRITICAL" vulns_report.txt; then
    echo "Critical vulnerabilities found! Failing the build."
    exit 1
fi
```

This script performs severity-filtered scans during build stages, aborting deployments if critical risks are detected, thereby enforcing security gates.

- **Automate vulnerability scanning** at every stage-from development to deployment-to detect issues early.

- **Maintain up-to-date vulnerability databases** and synchronize them continuously with scanning tools.

- **Use dependency version pinning** to reduce variability in vulnerability exposure and simplify update tracking.

- **Integrate vulnerability reports** with centralized issue trackers for triage, prioritization, and accountability.

- **Standardize patch workflows** including automated rebuilds, test validations, and secure rollout strategies.

- **Perform post-deployment verification** to ensure patches are effective and no new risks arise.

Applying these practices consistently ensures that security risks associated with chart dependencies and container images are managed proactively, sustaining resilience across the software supply chain.

8.3. Enforcing Compliance via Helm Charts

Helm charts provide a powerful mechanism for managing Kubernetes application deployments through templated resource definitions and parameterized configurations. To enforce organizational and regulatory compliance during deployment, it is essential to integrate policy enforcement mechanisms directly into Helm-based pipelines. This ensures that compliance validations occur automatically and transparently at deploy time, reducing drift and minimizing manual intervention.

The integration of admission controllers, Open Policy Agent (OPA) policies, and compliance-as-code frameworks within Helm pipelines establishes a robust compliance governance model. Admission controllers are Kubernetes-native hooks that intercept requests to the Kubernetes API server, making them the natural enforcement points for static policy checks and dynamic validation. Meanwhile, OPA offers a flexible, declarative language (Rego) to author fine-grained policies that react to live resource configurations. Compliance-as-code translates regulatory and internal compliance mandates into executable declarative policies and validations that can be integrated within CI/CD pipelines.

A fundamental approach is to establish admission controllers configured with OPA Gatekeeper or OPA's Kubernetes admission control webhook to enforce compliance policies automatically on all Helm-driven deployments. Gatekeeper facilitates constraint templates mapped to Rego policies, providing customizable and extensible policy enforcement. When a Helm deployment is initiated using `helm install` or `helm upgrade`, the manifest rendered by the Helm templating engine is submitted to the Kubernetes API server. At this juncture, admission controller webhooks intercept the request and evaluate it against pre-configured OPA constraints. Any violation-such as improper labeling, disallowed container images, or insufficient resource limits-results in admission rejection, thus ensuring no non-compliant resource is persisted.

Integrating these validations into the CI/CD pipeline enables early detection of compliance issues. A typical pipeline might render the Helm chart manifests in a build or test stage using `helm template`, then pass the resulting manifests to `conftest` for policy evaluation. Conftest uses OPA policies to statically analyze Kubernetes YAML before deployment. This combination allows an organization to shift compliance detection left, identifying violations prior to direct cluster interaction.

```
helm template myapp ./myapp-chart --values values.yaml > rendered
    .yaml
conftest test rendered.yaml
```

```
PASS  Pod myapp-pod compliance checks
FAIL  Deployment myapp-deployment resource-limits
```

The failed output informs developers precisely which resource attributes violate policies, linking code changes to compliance results effectively. This closure of feedback loops accelerates remediation and increases developer accountability.

Compliance-as-code extends beyond the enforcement in cluster and basic CI stages by codifying regulatory controls such as PCI-DSS, HIPAA, GDPR, or internal standards into constraint libraries. These can be imported into pipeline repositories and composed modularly as per organizational mandate. For example, resource quotas, secure context constraints, audit logging requirements, and image provenance scanning policies can be simultaneously managed through reusable OPA constraint templates.

To illustrate, consider a constraint template enforcing container image provenance, ensuring images originate only from approved registries. This Rego snippet enforces a strict image source whitelist:

```
package k8svalidations

deny[msg] {
  input.kind.kind == "Pod"
  container := input.spec.containers[_]
  not startswith(container.image, "registry.company.com/")
  msg := sprintf("Unapproved image registry in %v: %v", [input.
    metadata.name, container.image])
}
```

By coupling these constraints with Helm workflows, each deployment inherently verifies image compliance. Gatekeeper's audit capability then produces cluster-wide compliance reports, so operators gain continuous visibility of policy adherence.

Moreover, Helm charts themselves can be constructed to encapsulate compliance checks by embedding metadata annotations and labels consistent with regulatory frameworks. For example, automated inclusion of labels like `compliance.kubernetes.io/pci-dss: "true"` and enforced semantic versioning reflect traceability and auditability. Parameter validation can be added to Helm's `values.yaml` schema, rejecting unauthorized configurations such as overly permissive RBAC settings during chart installation time via `helm lint` and custom validation hooks.

Organizations adopting infrastructure as code best practices benefit from embedding compliance constraints directly into Helm charts and their deployment pipelines, achieving continuous compliance assurance without sacrificing agility. Integrations with tooling such as `helm unittest` for pre-deployment validation, and use of policy-as-code scanning in pull request workflows, act as quality gates before Kubernetes accepts any resources.

The orchestrated mechanism incorporating admission controllers, OPA policies, and compliance-as-code yields a multi-layered enforcement model:

- **Pre-deployment Validation:** Static analysis of Helm manifests against compliance policies before cluster interaction.

- **Admission-time Enforcement:** Dynamic request evaluation by Kubernetes admission webhooks rejecting non-compliant resources.

- **Continuous Auditing:** Periodic compliance scans and reporting to detect drift or unauthorized changes within live clusters.

Such an architecture ensures that organizational and regulatory compliance is verifiably met at deploy time, facilitating governance automation and enabling rapid, secure application delivery within Kubernetes environments. This convergence of declarative policy, programmable admission control, and templated deployment pipelines is foundational to modern secure Kubernetes operations.

8.4. Auditing and Forensics in Kubernetes and Helm

Effective auditing and forensic capabilities in Kubernetes and Helm are essential for maintaining a secure and compliant environment. They enable incident detection, rapid investigation, and post-event analysis. The multifaceted nature of Kubernetes clusters, combined with the abstraction introduced by Helm, requires a comprehensive approach to logging, API call auditing, and workflow tracing that captures sufficient detail while maintaining performance and manageability.

Logging forms the fundamental data source for forensic investigations and auditing trails. Kubernetes components, including the API server, controller manager, scheduler, kubelets, and container runtime, generate critical logs reflecting cluster operations, decisions, and errors. Additionally, application-level logs provide insights into workload behavior.

Centralizing these logs is imperative to enable correlation and efficient search. A typical logging pipeline employs agents such as `Fluentd` or `Fluent Bit` deployed as DaemonSets to collect logs from all nodes. Logs are forwarded to scalable backends like Elasticsearch or cloud-native services such as Amazon CloudWatch or Google Cloud Logging.

To enhance forensic value, logs must be timestamped with synchronized cluster-wide clock references (e.g., NTP or chrony), ensuring accurate event sequencing. Metadata enrichment-injecting Kubernetes context such as Pod name, namespace, container ID, and node-facilitates precise event correlation.

```
kubectl apply -f https://raw.githubusercontent.com/fluent/fluent-
    bit-kubernetes-logging/master/fluent-bit-daemonset.yaml
```

Log retention policies must reflect compliance requirements and forensic needs, typically balancing data availability for 30 to 90 days. Immutable storage or append-only systems strengthen the integrity and non-repudiation of logs.

The Kubernetes API server acts as the central management plane, with all cluster operations channeled through its RESTful interface. Auditing API calls provides visibility into who accessed or modified cluster resources and the nature of those interactions.

Configuring the API auditing subsystem involves enabling the audit feature in the API server manifest with policy files that define which events to capture and how to categorize them based on verb, resource, user identity, and other attributes. Audit policies can be fine-tuned to reduce noise by filtering read-only requests or system internal calls while maintaining coverage of changes and sensitive operations.

Example audit policy snippet:

```
apiVersion: audit.k8s.io/v1
kind: Policy
rules:
- level: Metadata
  verbs: ["create", "update", "patch", "delete"]
  resources:
  - group: ""
    resources: ["secrets", "pods", "configmaps"]
- level: None
  verbs: ["get", "list", "watch"]
```

Audit logs typically include request and response timestamps, user identifiers (via client certificates or tokens), HTTP status codes, source IPs, and affected resource details. Secure and scalable log storage for audit records is critical; many operators forward audit logs to external syslog servers or dedicated SIEMs (Security Information and Event Management).

Helm's templating and release management introduce an additional abstraction layer, which must be thoroughly audited to avoid blind spots. Helm commands and resource changes triggered during chart installations, upgrades, or rollbacks should be logged and correlated with Kubernetes audit events.

With Helm 3, releases leverage Secrets or ConfigMaps within the target namespace to store release metadata. Monitoring changes to these resources can provide indirect visibility into the Helm-driven deployment lifecycle. However, this approach alone is insufficient for comprehensive auditing.

To achieve robust Helm workflow tracing, integrate command audit logging at the CI/CD platform or operator terminal level where Helm commands are executed. Additionally, consider adopting Helm plugins or wrappers that record and transmit detailed Helm activity.

Supporting Helm audit trails with cognitive correlation against the Kubernetes audit logs validates the integrity and timing of deployment workflows. Forensic investigations benefit from reconstructing the entire sequence: Helm release command, resulting Kubernetes API calls, and subsequent application log entries.

Complex cloud-native environments often involve multi-component, multi-namespace workflows. Workflow tracing extends auditing by correlating actions across different layers and components, thus providing end-to-end visibility.

Tracing tools such as `OpenTelemetry` or `Jaeger` can be integrated to capture and propagate context identifiers through Kubernetes workloads, Helm lifecycle events, and API calls. Injecting trace IDs into logs and audit events enables stitching disparate data sources into coherent investigative timelines.

Deployment of sidecar proxies or instrumentation within containers facilitates this data capture without intrusive code changes, which is critical for post-mortem root cause analysis in microservice architectures.

Robust auditing capabilities form a cornerstone of regulatory compliance frameworks (e.g., PCI DSS, HIPAA, GDPR) when operating Kubernetes clusters. Defensible evidence requires logs and audit data to be:

- Collected consistently and securely without gaps,

- Protected against unauthorized modification or deletion through encryption, access controls, and immutability,

- Correlated and retained according to defined policies,

- Regularly reviewed and verified via automated tooling or human audit,

- Supported by documented processes for incident investigation and escalation.

Leveraging Infrastructure as Code (IaC) to declare and enforce auditing configurations enhances reproducibility and reduces drift. Continuous monitoring tools can alert on suspicious patterns derived from audit logs, such as unauthorized access attempts, privilege escalations, or anomalous Helm releases.

Implementing comprehensive auditing and forensics in Kubernetes and Helm involves orchestrated efforts:

- Enable Kubernetes API server audit logging with tailored policy files to focus on critical resources and operations.

- Deploy centralized logging agents cluster-wide, ensuring logs from all components and workloads are collected with rich metadata.

- Include Helm command and release change tracking by integrating audit logs from Helm operators and correlating with Kubernetes events.

- Employ distributed tracing technologies to link disparate events and workflows for coherent forensic narratives.

- Secure log storage and retention configurations to align with compliance mandates and maintain chain-of-custody.

Such a holistic approach equips security architects and cluster operators with forensic readiness and incident response agility, critically supporting cloud-native security governance and compliance programs.

8.5. Chart Review and Release Gatekeeping Processes

The stability and security of production environments hinge on robust chart review, approval, and security testing mechanisms established prior to code deployment. Structured gatekeeping functions as a critical safeguard, ensuring that every change introduced through release cycles meets stringent quality and compliance standards while maintaining alignment with organizational policies.

A foundational aspect of the gatekeeping workflow is the formalized chart review process. Helm charts, representing Kubernetes application packaging, necessitate meticulous validation to assure consistency, configurability, and adherence to best practices. Automated and manual review stages should be integrated to verify chart syntax, semantic correctness of templating, and configuration parameter constraints. Static analysis tools customized for Helm charts, such as `helm lint` combined with custom schema validators, can identify common misconfigurations, security antipatterns, and deprecated API usage. However, automated diagnostics alone do not suffice; domain experts must validate architectural decisions reflected in chart templates, resource requests, and environment-specific overrides to prevent runtime failures and performance regressions.

Approval workflows must be designed to enforce accountability and traceability throughout the release pipeline. A pull request (PR) based model utilizing version control systems (e.g., Git) establishes a transparent audit trail, where code reviewers validate proposed modifications against defined acceptance criteria. Multi-level approvals are recommended for high-impact components, involving platform owners, security teams, and performance engineers. Incorporating automated checks such as Continuous Integration (CI) pipelines that run Helm tests, integration tests, and compliance scanners ensures that only charts passing all gates proceed further. The approval mechanism should integrate with ticketing or change management systems to link code changes to broader operational incidents or feature requests, enabling holistic oversight.

Security testing forms a pivotal pillar of production readiness validation. Chart artifacts must undergo both static and dynamic security analyses. Static Application Security Testing (SAST) tools can analyze Helm charts for manifest vulnerabilities including misconfigured RBAC roles, insecure container privileges, or exposure of sensitive data in environment variables and config maps. Additionally, security policy enforcement frameworks like Open Policy Agent (OPA) Gatekeeper can be embedded within the cluster to enforce policy-as-code rules. Dynamic testing involves deploying the chart to isolated staging or test environments for runtime vulnerability scanning and behavioral analysis. Container security scanners inspect included images for known Common Vulnerabilities and Exposures (CVEs), whereas network policy verifications confirm that inter-service communication complies with least privilege principles.

Establishing rigorous guardrails leverages enforcement of policy-driven automation to preempt security and stability issues. For example, pre-commit hooks and branch protection rules can block merges unless all associated linting, testing, and security checks complete successfully. Deployment pipelines configured with environment-specific validation steps minimize human error and deliver predictable deployment outcomes. Observability tools monitoring resource utilization, application logs, and security events in test environments provide early indicators of potential issues, enabling iterative refinement before production rollout.

The gatekeeping process must also consider versioning and rollback strategies to mitigate risk in face of production anomalies. Semantic versioning of Helm charts, coupled with immutable artifact repositories, guarantees reproducibility and traceability of deployed releases. Automated rollback procedures triggered by health checks or custom alerting policies ensure rapid restoration to known good states, thereby reducing service disruption during unexpected faults.

Integrating chart review and release gatekeeping into the broader DevSecOps lifecycle promotes a culture of proactive quality and security validation. Shared ownership models between developers, platform engineers, and security teams foster continuous improvement of review criteria and testing coverage. Metrics derived from gatekeeper activities-such as defect detection rates, approval cycle times, and security scan results-provide actionable insights for refining release process efficiency.

Establishing structured chart review, approval workflows, and comprehensive security testing creates a rigorous barrier against unstable or non-compliant deployments. These processes function as essential guardrails ensuring stability and enforcing organizational policies, effectively controlling the quality of code introduction into production. Through integration of automation, policy enforcement, and collaborative governance, gatekeeping mechanisms transition from reactive checkpoints into proactive enablers of reliable software delivery at scale.

8.6. Secure Supply Chain for Helm Charts

Ensuring the integrity and authenticity of Helm charts is paramount in securing Kubernetes deployments from supply chain attacks. The supply chain for Helm charts encompasses multiple stages, including chart creation, packaging, repository hosting, distribution, and deployment. To achieve end-to-end security, it is essential to incorporate mechanisms that validate chart sources, digitally sign chart artifacts, and verify provenance before deployment, thereby preventing malicious or tampered charts from compromising cluster environments.

Chart Source Validation

The initial step in a secure Helm supply chain is rigorous validation of the source code and templates used to generate charts. Chart developers must maintain best practices such as:

- **Source Code Repository Integrity:** Use version-controlled systems (e.g., Git) with branch protection, signed commits, and audit trails to prevent unauthorized modifications.

- **Static Analysis:** Employ automated static analysis tools on Helm templates and values files to detect insecure patterns and possible injection vectors.

- **Dependency Verification:** Ensure all chart dependencies are explicitly defined and resolved from trusted origins, avoiding transitive dependencies from unknown sources.

These measures, using cryptographically verifiable repositories and continuous integration, guard against code-level compromises before packaging.

Signing Helm Chart Artifacts

After chart packaging, the next critical security control is signing the Helm chart archive. Helm uses the Chart.yaml metadata file, which defines the chart version and dependencies, but the archive files are themselves unsigned by default. To address this, artifact signing attaches a cryptographic signature to chart files, enabling recipients to verify origin and integrity. This is typically performed via:

- **PGP/GPG Signatures:** Chart maintainers sign the packaged chart .tgz files using private keys. Helm clients can verify these signatures using the corresponding public keys before installation.

- **Use of Notary or CT Logs:** Integration with The Update Framework (TUF) or certificate transparency logs adds additional layers of trust and auditability.

Example command to sign a chart artifact using GPG:

```
helm package redis-chart/
gpg --armor --detach-sign redis-chart-1.0.0.tgz
helm verify redis-chart-1.0.0.tgz
```

The helm verify command checks the signature against locally trusted public keys, rejecting unsigned or tampered charts.

Provenance and Integrity Checks

Provenance metadata tracks the origin and transformation history of a Helm chart, facilitating transparency and accountability in the supply chain. Provenance files accompanying packaged charts typically contain:

- Chart metadata including version, maintainer info, and source repository URLs

- Checksums and cryptographic hashes of the archive files

- Signature data and key identifiers used in signing

Verification of provenance involves confirming that the chart package matches these metadata assertions, detecting any modifications since signing. Helm's built-in provenance verification can be invoked using:

```
helm verify stable/nginx-1.2.0.tgz
```

which outputs either confirmation of validity or explicit error messages indicating potential tampering.

Use of Trusted Helm Repositories

Securing the distribution phase requires hosting Helm charts on trusted, secured repositories. Best practices include:

- **Access Control:** Enforce authentication and authorization mechanisms to control who can publish or update charts.

- **Transport Security:** Enable TLS to prevent man-in-the-middle attacks during chart downloads.

- **Repository Signing:** Utilize signing mechanisms on entire repositories, not just individual charts, to provide aggregate trust.

- **Content Scanning:** Integrate vulnerability scanners and policy enforcement engines to detect malicious or vulnerable content before publication.

Popular Helm repositories such as Artifact Hub provide signing and provenance capabilities, as well as integration points for policy enforcement tools.

Automated Verification in CI/CD Pipelines

To operationalize end-to-end security, continuous integration and deployment pipelines must automatically enforce validation and verification steps. This includes:

- Automatically verifying chart signatures and provenance before deploying charts to clusters.

- Rejecting charts that fail integrity or authenticity checks.

- Incorporating supply chain security tools such as `cosign`, `notary`, or `sigstore` for signing and verification workflows.

- Logging and alerting on verification failures to enable rapid incident response.

These steps prevent unauthorized or compromised charts from being deployed, reducing risk exposure.

Runtime Policy Enforcement

Even with rigorous source and artifact validation, runtime defense layers provide additional assurance. Kubernetes admission controllers and tools such as `OPA Gatekeeper` or `Kyverno` can:

- Enforce signature and provenance validation at install time, rejecting unsigned or unverified charts.

- Implement compliance policies that restrict the usage of untrusted chart repositories.

- Monitor deployed charts for drift from their verified state, flagging anomalies.

This defense-in-depth approach ensures that only authenticated, verified Helm charts manifest within production environments.

A secure Helm chart supply chain relies on layered cryptographic protections spanning source validation, artifact signing, provenance verification, trusted distribution, automated CI/CD checks, and runtime enforcement policies. By embedding cryptographic signatures and provenance metadata into the Helm chart ecosystem, organizations achieve end-to-end assurance that only authentic, untampered charts are deployed. Integration with public key infrastructures, transparency logs, and supply chain security frameworks elevates trust while minimizing attack surfaces. This comprehensive model significantly mitigates risks posed by supply chain compromise in Kubernetes application delivery.

Chapter 9

Helm at Scale: Multi-Tenancy, Performance, and Troubleshooting

Scaling Helm isn't just about managing more releases—it's about designing for separation, resilience, and debuggability in environments where hundreds of teams and thousands of deployments co-exist. This chapter reveals proven patterns for multi-tenancy, fine-grained resource isolation, and smooth troubleshooting, empowering you to stretch Helm's capabilities without losing control or visibility. Whether you're running a massive platform or supporting diverse workloads, discover how Helm scales to meet enterprise demands.

9.1. Designing Charts for Multi-Tenancy and Reusability

Deploying Helm charts in environments where multiple teams and products coexist demands a rigorous design approach to ensure strict namespace boundaries, flexible customizations, and parameterization. Achieving multi-tenancy and reusability effectively reduces duplicated effort, enforces isolation, and simplifies maintenance across the organization. To this end, several strategies must be considered when designing charts that are intended for use in diverse, shared Kubernetes clusters.

Enforcing Namespace Isolation through Templates and Values

A fundamental principle for multi-tenancy is that each tenant operates within an isolated namespace to prevent resource conflicts and security leaks. Helm charts must therefore be constructed to avoid hardcoding namespaces. Instead, the namespace is typically specified at installation or upgrade time using a parameterized value combined with template functions.

For example, rather than statically defining metadata fields as:

```
metadata:
  namespace: default
```

charts should utilize either Helm's built-in `.Release.Namespace` or a custom value:

```
metadata:
  namespace: {{ .Values.namespace | default .Release.Namespace }}
```

This approach allows Helm users to assign the target namespace explicitly through the `--namespace` flag or override `.Values.namespace` in their `values.yaml`, thereby enforcing separation. It also supports scenarios where a single chart is deployed multiple times in distinct namespaces, each representing different tenants or environments.

Further, namespacing must extend beyond just the `metadata.namespace` field. Labels, annotations, resource names, and Role-Based Access Control (RBAC) bindings should also be parameterized to reflect namespace scoping accurately, ensuring no inadvertent cross-tenant access. For instance, cluster-scoped resources must be designed with tenant-specific identifiers, such as a name prefix or label selector tied to the namespace parameter.

Parameterizing for Flexibility and Control

Reusability relies heavily on parameterization. A well-designed `values.yaml` file exposes configuration options spanning resource sizes, replica counts, image versions, feature toggles, and ingress rules. This allows different teams or environments-staging, production, development-to adapt deployments without modifying the chart's templates.

Design principles for parameterization include:

- **Logical Grouping:** Organize values hierarchically to differentiate between common settings and tenant-specific overrides. For example:

```
global:
  imagePullPolicy: IfNotPresent

tenant:
  namespace: my-tenant
  replicas: 3
```

- **Defaults and Overrides:** Provide sensible defaults in `values.yaml` to facilitate developer onboarding and quick iteration, while allowing overrides via `helm install -f` or `--set` for tenant-specific deployments.

- **Validation and Constraints:** Although Helm does not natively support schema validation, techniques such as JSON schema validation or custom pre-install hooks can enforce value sanity. Parameters should be constrained to acceptable ranges or formats to avoid deployment failures or security risks.

- **Avoiding Hardcoded Secrets or Credentials:** Parameter references to secrets should rely on external Kubernetes Secrets or ConfigMaps to maintain separation of concerns and safeguard sensitive data.

Template Modularity and Use of Named Templates

To maximize reusability, charts should employ a modular template architecture. Reusable snippets are defined as named templates using Helm's – define directive. These templates can accept parameters and be included as needed, fostering consistency and reducing duplication.

For instance, a named template for a standardized container definition might look like:

```
{{- define "mychart.container" -}}
name: {{ .name }}
image: {{ .image.repository }}:{{ .image.tag }}
ports:
  - containerPort: {{ .port }}
{{- end }}
```

Then invoked within the main pod spec:

```
containers:
  - {{- template "mychart.container" dict "name" "app" "image" .
    Values.image "port" 8080 }}
```

This modularization simplifies maintaining charts that serve multiple products or teams, as updates to shared patterns propagate automatically. It becomes easier to implement tenant-specific logic through conditional blocks or parameter-driven branching, preserving the single source of truth principle.

Supporting Multi-Tenant Ingress and Service Exposure

Charts should also accommodate diverse networking requirements for multi-tenancy, such as isolated ingress paths, hostnames, or load balancer configurations. Parameterizing ingress resources allows tenants to specify their domain names and TLS secrets without chart modification. For example:

```
ingress:
  enabled: true
  hosts:
    - host: {{ .Values.tenant.ingressHost }}
      paths:
        - /
  tls:
    - secretName: {{ .Values.tenant.tlsSecret }}
      hosts:
        - {{ .Values.tenant.ingressHost }}
```

When multiple tenants share the same cluster, routing conflicts and security policies must be carefully addressed. Charts can support this by allowing ingress annotations or custom labels to be overridden, ensuring compatibility with ingress controllers or service meshes.

For internal services, the chart should namespace Service names and port mappings with tenant context. If cross-tenant service discovery occurs, explicit naming conventions help avoid collision and unauthorized access.

Chart Dependencies with Tenant-Aware Isolation

Complex products often consist of multiple Helm charts, with dependencies modeled in `Chart.yaml` via the `dependencies` field. When designing for multi-tenancy, dependency charts should also follow strict namespace scoping and be parameterized accordingly.

Helm's dependency update and requirements management commands provide mechanisms to synchronize subcharts, but tenant-specific overrides must be propagated down correctly. Leveraging `.Values` hierarchy allows the parent chart to inject tenant parameters into subcharts:

```
dependencies:
  - name: common-library
    version: 1.2.3
```

```
    repository: https://example.com/charts

# In values.yaml
common-library:
  namespace: {{ .Values.tenant.namespace }}
  replicaCount: 2
```

This design ensures that subcomponents remain tenant-aware and
prevents cross-tenant leakage through cluster-scoped resources
managed by dependencies.

**Avoiding Side Effects and Cluster-Scoped Resource Con-
flicts**

Developers must exercise caution when including cluster-scoped
resources in multi-tenant charts. Resources such as ClusterRoles,
ClusterRoleBindings, or CustomResourceDefinitions (CRDs) are
potentially shared across all namespaces, which can undermine
tenant isolation if hardcoded or unmanaged.

Strategies to mitigate this include:

- Separating cluster-scoped components into dedicated charts
  with controlled installation procedures, possibly managed by
  cluster operators rather than tenants.

- Using tenant-specific naming conventions for cluster-scoped
  resources, where feasible.

- Deferring critical RBAC policies to be managed outside tenant charts, leveraging namespaces' Roles and RoleBindings
  for intra-tenant access control.

Comprehensively documenting these constraints guides teams on
the limitations and best practices when deploying the charts in
multi-tenant environments.

Versioning and Distribution for Shared Usage

Reusability across teams and products also relies on robust versioning and distribution strategies. Helm charts designed for

multi-tenancy should adhere to semantic versioning conventions, clearly specifying breaking changes, enhancements, and patches.

Publishing charts in centralized Helm repositories accessible to all relevant teams ensures standardized usage. Employing continuous integration and delivery (CI/CD) pipelines to automatically validate, package, and release charts promotes quality and reduces integration risks.

Teams can then pin desired chart versions in their workflows, facilitating controlled upgrades and rollbacks specific to tenant deployments without affecting others.

Charts supporting multi-tenancy and reusability require deliberate architectural choices focused on namespace parameterization, modular templates, and flexible customization. Enforcing strict isolation boundaries, exposing tenant-aware configuration, and carefully handling cluster-scoped resources result in Helm charts that can be safely and efficiently shared across organizations. Such disciplined design not only promotes collaboration but also strengthens security and operational stability in complex Kubernetes environments.

9.2. Namespace and Resource Isolation

Kubernetes provides a powerful abstraction for multi-tenant environments through the concept of namespaces, which logically partition cluster resources and enable resource isolation within a shared cluster. Effective namespace and resource isolation are critical to preventing contention, avoiding accidental conflicts, and ensuring security boundaries among multiple users or teams. This section explores the mechanisms Kubernetes offers—namespaces, resource quotas, and Helm's naming conventions—to enforce isolation, protect tenants from noisy neighbors, and minimize errors caused by overlapping resource definitions.

At the core of Kubernetes resource isolation lies the *namespace*, a
virtual cluster backed by the same physical cluster infrastructure.
Namespaces create isolated scopes for Kubernetes resources such
as Pods, Services, ConfigMaps, and Secrets, thus segmenting workloads and access control domains. By default, a Kubernetes cluster
provides a `default` namespace, but multi-tenant implementations
should create dedicated namespaces for each tenant or workload
group to enforce separation.

Namespaces alone cannot restrict resource consumption; they
serve only as scopes. To limit resource usage and prevent resource
exhaustion by any single tenant, *ResourceQuotas* must be configured within each namespace. ResourceQuota objects define constraints on resources including CPU, memory, object counts, and
persistent volume claims. For example, quotas can cap the number
of Pods or the aggregate CPU request in a namespace, ensuring no
tenant can monopolize cluster resources. A typical ResourceQuota
YAML specification resembles:

```
apiVersion: v1
kind: ResourceQuota
metadata:
  name: compute-resources
  namespace: tenant-a
spec:
  hard:
    pods: "10"
    requests.cpu: "4"
    requests.memory: 8Gi
    limits.cpu: "8"
    limits.memory: 16Gi
```

This object tightly bounds tenant `tenant-a`'s resource consumption. If a user attempts to schedule Pods exceeding these limits, Kubernetes will reject them, enforcing isolation at the cluster scheduler level.

Namespaces also facilitate *access control* boundaries by integrating with Role-Based Access Control (RBAC). Defining Roles and
RoleBindings within a namespace limits a user or service account's
privileges strictly to resources within that namespace, preventing

unauthorized cross-tenant access. This mechanism complements resource isolation by enforcing logical separation of privileges, reducing the risk of accidental or malicious interference.

Effective naming conventions are also essential to avoid resource clashes and to simplify management in multi-tenant clusters. Helm, the Kubernetes package manager, encourages a systematic scheme that incorporates a *release name* as a unique prefix for all resources it deploys. This convention reduces the likelihood of resource collisions when multiple Helm releases coexist in the same namespace or across namespaces. Helm templates commonly prefix resource names with {{ .Release.Name }}- to guarantee uniqueness. For instance:

```
apiVersion: apps/v1
kind: Deployment
metadata:
  name: {{ .Release.Name }}-web
  namespace: {{ .Release.Namespace }}
spec:
  replicas: 3
  ...
```

Following this pattern systematically prevents accidental overrides of one tenant's resources by another's deployments, an important safeguard in clusters shared by multiple Helm releases.

Beyond straightforward uniqueness, Helm's release names can serve as tenant identifiers, enabling operators to link deployed objects to their owners and to audit or troubleshoot accordingly. Leveraging Helm charts with consistent naming also facilitates resource lifecycle management, as Helm tracks changes and orchestrates upgrades or rollbacks without impacting other deployments.

Resource isolation must be complemented by monitoring and alerting mechanisms that detect *noisy neighbor* behavior—where a tenant's workload adversely impacts others' performance by excessive resource consumption or misconfiguration. Kubernetes metrics servers, Prometheus, and custom resource metrics can help enforce quotas proactively by triggering alerts on nearing re-

source limits. When combined with automated remediation or
scaling, these tools promote cluster stability and fairness.

Finally, careful policy definition and governance processes are necessary to maintain namespace hygiene over time. Periodic audits
of namespaces, ResourceQuotas, and Helm release inventories can
detect stale or orphaned resources. Automated cleanup scripts
or namespace deletion policies prevent resource leakage and reduce resource starvation risks. In environments with frequent tenant churn, ephemeral namespaces verified through admission controllers can strengthen tenant lifecycle management.

Namespaces provide essential logical partitioning within Kubernetes, but enforcing strict resource and operational isolation requires combining namespaces with well-defined ResourceQuotas
and access boundaries via RBAC. Helm's naming conventions further reduce accidental interference, enabling safe coexistence of
multiple tenants' workloads. Adhering to these best practices ensures cluster resources are fairly allocated, tenants remain insu-
lated from noisy neighbors, and operational risks due to resource
collisions are minimized—forming a robust foundation for scalable
and secure multi-tenant Kubernetes deployments.

9.3. Helm Performance Optimizations

Helm, as the de facto package manager for Kubernetes, plays a pivotal role in the deployment pipeline of cloud-native applications.
However, in large-scale environments, the rendering of charts and
the subsequent installation of applications can introduce significant latency and resource consumption, thereby affecting the overall efficiency of Continuous Integration and Continuous Deployment (CI/CD) workflows. This section delves into profiling and
tuning techniques aimed at optimizing Helm performance to reduce both runtime and resource demands during the chart rendering and installation phases.

Profiling the rendering process in Helm involves template rendering combined with value substitution, producing Kubernetes manifest files to be applied to the cluster. Profiling this phase begins with isolating the rendering workload from the cluster interaction, which enables targeted analysis.

The `helm template` command is instrumental for this purpose:

```
helm template <release-name> <chart-path> --values <values-file>
    --debug --output-dir ./rendered
```

This command outputs rendered manifests locally without invoking the Kubernetes API, allowing measurement of rendering time independently. Tools such as `time` can be used to benchmark:

```
time helm template myrelease ./mychart
```

Profiling results often reveal that complex templates with deeply nested control structures and functions increase CPU usage and latency. In charts containing many templates or extensive use of helper templates (via `_helpers.tpl`), it is advisable to analyze and simplify the Go templating logic.

The `helm lint` command with the `--strict` flag can help detect deprecated APIs or inefficient constructs impacting performance indirectly during rendering:

```
helm lint ./mychart --strict
```

Furthermore, Helm's internal profiling can be extended by building Helm from source with custom instrumentation, although such efforts are typically reserved for organizations needing deep insight.

One of the primary levers for improving rendering performance is minimizing chart complexity:

- **Template Flattening**: Avoid overuse of nested `include` and `define` template functions. Wherever possible, flatten templates to reduce invocation overhead.

217

- **Conditional Logic Minimization**: Excessive conditional blocks (`if`/`else`) in templates not only impact render time but also complicate maintenance. Utilizing values with sensible defaults can reduce such conditions.

- **Limit Custom Functions**: Avoid computationally expensive custom functions in templates and prefer straightforward string and list manipulations.

- **Split Large Charts**: Breaking down monolithic charts into smaller, microservice-aligned subcharts can decrease rendering times by limiting the scope of the rendered templates per deployment.

Values used for templating have a significant impact on performance, especially when using large or deeply nested YAML structures. Techniques include:

- **Avoid Large Inline Values**: Passing large multi-line strings or complex arrays in `values.yaml` may degrade rendering speeds. Instead, use ConfigMaps or external references where feasible.

- **Precompute Values**: For dynamic but deterministic values, precompute values outside Helm and inject them via values files to minimize template logic.

- **Reduce Duplication**: Consolidate duplicate entries in values files to avoid unnecessary cycles within templates.

After rendering, Helm's `install` or `upgrade` commands interact with Kubernetes API servers, applying the rendered manifests. In large clusters, API throttling, network latency, and cluster size can introduce substantial delays.

Profiling tools such as `kubectl get events --watch` and Kubernetes audit logs provide insights into request latencies and failure modes during Helm installations. Helm itself exposes a verbose debug mode:

```
helm install myrelease ./mychart --debug --wait --timeout 10m
```

The `--wait` flag ensures Helm waits for all resources to be ready before completing, but can cause delays if pod readiness probes or init containers are slow.

Performance optimization for installation includes:

- **Parallelizing Resource Creation**: Helm processes resources sequentially by default. Leveraging the experimental `--atomic` or plugin-based parallel installers can accelerate deployments by creating resources concurrently when safe.

- **Selective Resource Management**: For large charts, selectively installing only changed resources via the `--dry-run` and diffing tools helps avoid unnecessary API calls.

- **Resource Quota Awareness**: Ensuring cluster resource quotas align with expected loads prevents repeated installation failures and retries.

- **Timeout and Retry Tuning**: Adjusting Helm timeouts and retry policies based on cluster characteristics avoids long blocking states.

Caching rendered manifests and Helm chart dependencies reduces redundant computations in pipeline executions:

- **Pre-render Manifests**: In CI pipelines, pre-rendering manifests and storing them as artifacts permits rapid deployment phases without repeat rendering.

- **Helm Dependency Caching**: Using the `helm dependency update` command combined with local cache directories prevents repeated chart downloads.

- **Manifest Diffing**: Employ tools like `helm diff` plugin to detect changes and trigger deployments only when necessary, reducing unnecessary cluster API load.

When deploying to large clusters, resource usage on the client side can impede pipeline throughput:

- **Limit Helm Client Resources**: In automated environments, allocate sufficient CPU and memory to the Helm client process to avoid bottlenecks during rendering and API communication.

- **Offload Computation**: Consider offloading heavy chart operations to dedicated build agents or containerized environments isolated from pipeline control planes.

- **Logging and Monitoring**: Enable minimal yet sufficient logging to monitor Helm operations without incurring I/O overhead.

Establishing benchmarks for Helm rendering and installation durations is essential for measurable improvement. Integrate timing instrumentation into CI pipelines to capture Helm command runtimes, and correlate with cluster metrics to identify systemic bottlenecks.

An example script for benchmarking rendering time:

```
start=$(date +%s%N)
helm template myrelease ./mychart > /dev/null
end=$(date +%s%N)
elapsed=$(( (end - start) / 1000000 ))
echo "Rendering took: $elapsed ms"
```

Continuous profiling and iterative tuning guided by these metrics form the foundation for sustainable Helm performance optimizations in large-scale deployments.

Overall, Helm optimization requires a holistic approach spanning template simplification, strategic value management, installation tuning, and resource-conscious execution. The compounded improvements yield significant latency reductions and resource savings critical in pipeline workflows targeting substantial Kubernetes clusters.

9.4. Bulk Operations and Large-Scale Automation

Handling hundreds or thousands of software releases within an enterprise environment necessitates a systematic and scalable approach. The complexities introduced by volume, diversity of environments, and frequent update cycles render manual processes impractical and error-prone. To address these challenges, organizations turn to automation frameworks, scripting methodologies, and extension-based tooling that facilitate bulk upgrades, installations, and comprehensive reporting at scale.

Central to bulk operations is the principle of idempotency-the guarantee that repeated application of an operation yields the same system state without unintended side effects. Automation scripts and tools must be designed to recognize the current state of each deployed instance, allowing selective execution only for releases that require change, thus optimizing resource usage and minimizing downtime.

Scripting for Scalable Release Management

Scripting languages such as Python, Bash, or PowerShell serve as foundational instruments in bulk operations. By interfacing with APIs provided by package managers, deployment services, or orchestration platforms, scripts can query release statuses, trigger installation commands, and collate results into structured formats.

A typical bulk upgrade script performs the following sequence:

1. Enumerate all target systems or release identifiers, possibly

filtered by attributes such as environment, version, or component.

2. Retrieve current release versions and metadata to determine
   upgrade eligibility.

3. Execute parallel or sequential upgrade operations, carefully
   managing concurrency to avoid network saturation or resource contention.

4. Collect and log outcomes, classifying success, failure, and
   partial execution for subsequent review.

Proper error handling within scripts is crucial. Network interrup-
tions, dependency conflicts, or incompatible version constraints
can occur unpredictably. Implementing retries, fallback procedures, and alerting mechanisms enhances robustness and expe-
dites issue resolution.

```python
import concurrent.futures
import logging

def upgrade_release(target):
    try:
        current_version = query_version(target)
        if current_version < desired_version:
            result = perform_upgrade(target)
            return (target, 'Success', result)
        else:
            return (target, 'No Action', None)
    except Exception as e:
        return (target, 'Error', str(e))

targets = get_all_targets()
desired_version = '3.2.1'

with concurrent.futures.ThreadPoolExecutor(max_workers=20) as
        executor:
    results = executor.map(upgrade_release, targets)

for target, status, detail in results:
    logging.info(f"{target}: {status} - {detail}")
```

Automation Tooling and Orchestration Frameworks

While scripting provides flexibility, automation tooling offers structured, repeatable mechanisms packaged with advanced capabilities such as dependency resolution, state enforcement, and audit logging. Solutions like Ansible, Chef, Puppet, and SaltStack enable defining bulk operations as declarative playbooks or manifests.

In this context, bulk upgrades are modeled as idempotent tasks mapped to specific hosts or clusters. These tools utilize inventory management to categorize targets and support staged rollouts via groupings, ensuring safer deployments by limiting blast radius. Integration with Continuous Integration/Continuous Deployment (CI/CD) pipelines further automates release cycles, triggering bulk actions upon pipeline milestones.

Extending these frameworks with custom modules or plugins allows organization-specific logic, for example, preflight checks unique to a release type or specialized notification channels. The abstraction layers provided by these tools reduce manual intervention and improve transparency through detailed logs and return codes.

Extension Frameworks for Custom Bulk Operations

Many deployment ecosystems expose extension frameworks enabling customized bulk management tailored to domain-specific requirements. These extensions often manifest as SDKs, command-line tools, or RESTful services designed for enhanced scalability.

For instance, in package repository management systems, extension modules can facilitate bulk querying of release metadata, batch installations, or mass deprecations. By leveraging extension points, engineers can automate complex workflows like conditional rollbacks or graduated feature toggles across thousands of releases.

An effective extension design adheres to the principles of modularity and composability, permitting asynchronous execution and integration with external monitoring systems. Furthermore, exposing event hooks allows reactive automation where bulk operations trigger subsequent processes such as compliance scans or security audits.

Bulk Reporting and Monitoring at Scale

Automation of bulk operations must be complemented by scalable reporting frameworks capable of synthesizing results from distributed executions into actionable insights. Aggregated dashboards visualize upgrade statuses, failure modes, and temporal trends, facilitating rapid identification of systemic issues.

Common techniques include:

- Centralized logging systems (e.g., ELK Stack, Splunk) to ingest operation logs in real time.

- Time-series databases (e.g., Prometheus) to track health metrics and deployment frequencies.

- Automated report generation summarizing coverage, anomalies, and key performance indicators.

Effective monitoring enables proactive management, such as retargeting of upgrade jobs to failed nodes or prioritizing patches for vulnerable releases, thus closing the feedback loop in large-scale release stewardship.

Best Practices and Considerations

Automation at scale introduces considerations beyond pure technical implementation:

- **Security:** Credentials used in bulk operations require secure storage-vault technologies and ephemeral tokens minimize risk.

- **Change Control:** Coupling automation with rigorous version control and approval workflows prevents unauthorized or inconsistent releases.

- **Scalability:** Distributed architectures and load balancing avoid bottlenecks during concurrent operations.

- **Resilience:** Designing idempotent, retryable operations and employing circuit breakers prevent cascade failures.

- **Documentation:** Comprehensive operational documentation aids troubleshooting and knowledge transfer.

Incorporating these principles, organizations can evolve customized bulk operation frameworks that combine scripting agility, tooling strength, extensibility, and robust reporting. This infrastructure transforms large-scale release management from a logistical challenge into a predictable, controlled process aligned with enterprise agility and reliability goals.

9.5. Debugging Failed Releases and Diagnosing Drift

Effective management of Helm releases in Kubernetes environments necessitates the capability to systematically troubleshoot failed deployments and address configuration drift. Failures during Helm release operations often manifest through error messages that, if properly decoded, provide critical insight into the underlying issues. Configuration drift, indicating discrepancies between the desired state defined in Helm charts and the actual state observed in the cluster, can significantly hamper application stability and operational predictability. This section elucidates a methodical approach to diagnosing release failures and drift, enabling refined control over Helm-managed workloads.

When a Helm release fails, the immediate source of information is the error message produced by Helm's command-line interface. The `helm status` command reveals the release state, and `helm history` provides a timeline for release revisions. For detailed diagnostic data, the `helm get` command retrieves the manifest, hooks, and values for the release.

```
helm status <release-name>
helm history <release-name>
helm get manifest <release-name>
helm get hooks <release-name>
helm get values <release-name> --all
```

Common failure indicators include `timed out waiting for the condition`, `failed to create resource`, or forbidden access errors. Investigating Kubernetes events relevant to the release's namespace frequently exposes issues like resource quota breaches, RBAC constraints, or readiness probe failures. Commands such as the following are indispensable:

```
kubectl describe pod <pod-name> -n <namespace>
kubectl get events -n <namespace> --sort-by=.metadata.
    creationTimestamp
```

Advanced troubleshooting often involves inspecting pod logs for container-level errors. The command below extracts logs from a problematic pod:

```
kubectl logs <pod-name> -n <namespace> --all-containers=true
```

Failure patterns frequently resolve to insufficient resource allocation, manifest syntax errors, or incompatibility between chart specifications and cluster API versions. Therefore, validating the Helm templates using the `helm template` command can help isolate faulty manifest components prior to execution:

```
helm template <release-name> <chart-path> --values <values-file>
```

This local rendering previews Kubernetes manifests and permits static analysis using tools like `kubectl apply --dry-run=client`.

Configuration drift emerges when the cluster state diverges from the specifications defined in Helm chart values and manifests. This can result from manual edits, external controllers modifying resources, or failed reconciliation loops. Detecting drift requires reconciling the Helm release with the live cluster state.

The first step is to retrieve the live resource state with:

```
kubectl get all -l release=<release-name> -n <namespace> -o yaml
```

Comparing this output with the manifests used for the last successful Helm deployment reveals discrepancies. However, direct YAML diffing is error-prone due to Kubernetes' system-generated fields. A more resilient approach involves employing specialized tools like the `helm-diff` plugin, which integrates with Helm to provide side-by-side comparison of chart manifests and deployed resources:

```
helm plugin install https://github.com/databus23/helm-diff
helm diff upgrade <release-name> <chart-path> --values <values-
    file>
```

This command shows detailed differences, pinpointing exact fields where drift occurs.

Upon confirming drift, remediation proceeds either through Helm upgrades or manual intervention. The preferred method is to reapply the intended configuration via `helm upgrade` to restore the cluster to the chart-defined state:

```
helm upgrade <release-name> <chart-path> --values <values-file>
```

If the discrepancy results from external modifications (e.g., by operators or automated jobs), identifying and controlling or eliminating those external sources is crucial to maintaining consistency.

In cases where manual edits are unavoidable, it is advisable to adopt the `kubectl edit` or `kubectl patch` commands judiciously, followed by updating Helm values files and charts to reflect those accepted changes. This prevents the Helm reconciliation process from unintentionally overwriting manual adjustments.

```
kubectl edit deployment <deployment-name> -n <namespace>
kubectl patch svc <service-name> -p '{"spec":{"type":"NodePort
    "}}' -n <namespace>
```

In complex environments, implementing automated drift detection pipelines can reinforce cluster integrity. Integrating tools such
as Flux CD or Argo CD alongside Helm leverages continuous reconciliation and alerting for configuration deviations, thus preempt-
ing release failures due to unmanaged drift.

Systematic debugging benefits from awareness of frequent pitfalls:

- *Resource Quotas and Limits*: Overlooking namespace quotas often causes silent failures. Confirm quota availability
  before installation.

- *API Version Mismatches*: Helm charts using deprecated Kubernetes APIs may fail on newer clusters. Regularly update
  charts and test manifests for API compatibility.

- *Helm Hooks Failure*: Failure in lifecycle hooks (e.g., pre-
  install) will abort releases. Validate hooks independently
  and check hook execution logs.

- *Secrets and Sensitive Data*: Misconfigured secrets often
  cause deployment failures. Use external secrets management and carefully review access permissions.

- *Helm Release State Corruption*: Release metadata stored in
  ConfigMaps or Secrets may become inconsistent. The `helm
  rollback` or `helm uninstall --keep-history` commands
  can be employed cautiously.

Mastery of the interplay between Helm's declarative configuration,
Kubernetes' dynamic environment, and operational constraints
fosters robust troubleshooting. Consistent use of command-line
diagnostics, manifest previewing, and drift detection tools significantly reduces time to resolution of failed releases and prevents
persistent cluster state inconsistencies.

9.6. Helm Plugins and the Extension Ecosystem

Helm, as a robust package manager for Kubernetes, extends its capabilities beyond native commands through a flexible plugin system designed to augment functionality, streamline workflows, and tailor Helm's behavior to specific organizational requirements. This system leverages both first-party and third-party extensions, enabling users to optimize Helm's operational model without modifying the core codebase.

The Helm plugin architecture is based on simple conventions that allow users to create, install, and manage executable extensions. Each plugin is typically a standalone binary or script that implements a specific feature or workflow enhancement, receiving input via the command line and environment variables supplied by Helm itself. Plugins reside in a dedicated directory structure located by default in the user's environment under $HELM_HOME/plugins/, isolating them from core Helm binaries. This separation enhances maintainability and security by isolating third-party code from the Helm core.

A Helm plugin typically consists of a YAML metadata descriptor file plugin.yaml and one or more executable scripts or binaries. The descriptor outlines metadata fields such as the plugin's name, version, usage instructions, and the command(s) it provides. An example snippet of a plugin metadata file illustrates this structure:

```
name: plugin-example
version: 0.1.0
usage: "helm plugin-example [flags]"
description: "An example plugin to demonstrate Helm plugin
    structure"
command: "./plugin-example.sh"
```

Installation and management of plugins utilize Helm's built-in commands such as helm plugin install, helm plugin list, and helm plugin uninstall, enabling straightforward deployment and updates from remote repositories or local directories. For example, to install a plugin hosted on GitHub, the user executes:

```
helm plugin install https://github.com/example/helm-plugin-
    example
```

Once installed, the plugin commands integrate seamlessly into the Helm CLI interface, behaving as native subcommands, thus preserving user familiarity and reducing learning curves.

Key advantages of adopting Helm plugins include:

- **Feature Augmentation:** Plugins can provide capabilities not included in the core Helm command set, such as additional linting rules, customized chart validation, enhanced deployment diagnostics, or integration with external systems.

- **Workflow Automation:** Complex multi-step processes involving Helm operations and other toolchains can be automated inside plugins to enforce organizational standards and reduce human error.

- **Adaptability:** Specific operational requirements, such as naming conventions, deployment policies, or certificate management, can be encapsulated within plugins, avoiding fragmentation and ensuring consistency.

- **Community and Ecosystem Growth:** The Helm ecosystem benefits greatly from a vibrant community contributing plugins that address emerging use cases, share best practices, and support popular tools.

An illustrative example is `helm diff`, a widely adopted plugin that enables differential analysis between Helm releases or a release and its manifest files. This plugin helps users preview changes before applying upgrades, reducing risk and improving deployment confidence. Installation follows the standard flow:

```
helm plugin install https://github.com/databus23/helm-diff
```

After installation, users may invoke:

```
helm diff upgrade my-release ./my-chart
```

This produces a color-coded diff output that reveals differences in Kubernetes resource specifications.

Developers aiming to create custom plugins have multiple toolchain options:

- **Shell Scripts:** Simple plugin logic can be scripted in Bash or other shell environments, favoring rapid development and ease of modification.

- **Compiled Binaries:** For performance and distribution control, plugins can be written in Go or other compiled languages. Go is particularly suited given Helm itself is implemented in Go, facilitating use of Helm SDK libraries.

- **Language Wrappers:** Since plugins execute outside Helm, developers may use any language, allowing integration with existing ecosystems or internal tooling.

Best practices for plugin development emphasize minimizing side effects, maintaining idempotency where possible, and gracefully handling errors or missing dependencies. Plugin commands should adhere to the general Helm CLI conventions for flags and configuration options, propagating user parameters transparently to foster familiarity.

From an organizational perspective, a curated internal plugin repository enhances control and consistency. Companies can review, test, and certify plugins before deployment to production environments, thus ensuring conformance to security policies and operational standards. Helm's plugin installation commands support specifying explicit versions and signatures to improve supply chain security.

The Helm community maintains a curated plugin index, accessible through the Helm Hub and related registries, showcasing a breadth of extensions including but not limited to:

- `helm-unittest`: Provides unit testing capabilities for Helm charts, facilitating validation of chart templates and values.

- `helm-secrets`: Enables encryption and decryption of sensitive Helm chart values using tools such as Mozilla's SOPS.

- `helm-git`: Integrates Git operations for chart versioning within Helm workflows.

To integrate plugin functionality into Continuous Integration/Continuous Deployment (CI/CD) pipelines, automation systems invoke Helm commands augmented by these plugins, embedding additional validation, diffs, or security checks as part of release workflows. This underscores the importance of stable plugin APIs and semantic versioning to guarantee forward compatibility.

Overall, Helm's plugin system represents a fundamental pillar of extensibility within the Kubernetes package management landscape. By harnessing this ecosystem, organizations can tailor Helm to their nuanced needs, accelerate development lifecycles, and propagate uniform operational best practices across increasingly scaled Kubernetes deployments. The decoupled nature of plugins encourages innovation and community collaboration, driving continual enhancement of the Helm toolset.

Chapter 10

Future Directions and Innovations in Helm

Helm's evolution is shaped by a fast-moving cloud-native landscape, where innovation never stands still. This chapter peers ahead—exploring new standards, experimental delivery patterns, and cross-ecosystem integrations that promise to redefine how applications are delivered on Kubernetes. Whether you're an architect seeking strategic insight or a developer ready to embrace the frontier, discover what's next for Helm and how you can become a driver of the next wave of improvement.

10.1. Evolving Helm Standards and Chart Hub Ecosystem

Helm, as the de facto package manager for Kubernetes, continuously evolves to meet the growing complexity of cloud-native application deployment. Recent progress in Helm chart standards, authoring practices, and repository ecosystems reflects a maturation aligned with real-world operational challenges and scalability demands.

Fundamentally, Helm charts encapsulate Kubernetes manifests with templating and packaging capabilities. The latest Helm specification, formalized with version 3.8 and onwards, introduces refinements that standardize metadata, dependency handling, and validation mechanisms. A prominent advancement is the integration of stricter chart schema validation based on OpenAPI v3 schemas within `values.yaml`. This schema allows authors to declaratively specify value types, constraints, and allowed enumerations, streamlining validation during both chart installation and IDE-based authoring. It reduces runtime errors caused by misconfigured inputs and improves tooling interoperability.

The charts' `Chart.yaml` manifest manifests a heightened emphasis on semantic versioning aligned with the Semantic Versioning 2.0.0[1] specification, with explicit support for pre-release and build metadata tags to better reflect progressive development states. This facilitates more expressive versioning strategies for dependent charts and CI/CD workflows, ensuring safe upgrades and rollbacks in production environments. Additionally, Helm's dependency mechanism now supports transitive dependencies with explicit release condition flags and hooks, allowing conditional enablement of dependent subcharts without manual intervention. Such enhancements enable modular chart design, improving maintainability of large component stacks.

Beyond the core specification, evolving best practices have emerged from the community and the Helm maintainers to author charts emphasizing scalability, security, and usability. A principal tenet focuses on strict separation of concerns in chart templates by avoiding hard-coded values, maximizing configurability through `values.yaml`, and employing well-defined, typed input schemas. Chart authors are encouraged to leverage the new `.Capabilities` object extensively, which reflects

---

[1]https://semver.org/

234

Kubernetes cluster API versions, available resources, and Helm runtime environment to dynamically adjust manifests according to cluster capabilities. This yields charts resilient to differences across cloud providers and Kubernetes distributions.

Security-conscious chart authors now prioritize minimal privilege principles directly embedded in manifests. Default pod security contexts, RBAC policies, and container security settings declared in charts ensure compliance with organizational policies and Kubernetes Pod Security Standards. Furthermore, charts increasingly incorporate lifecycle hooks to handle complex upgrade scenarios, such as zero-downtime deployments and state migration, demonstrating a shift from simplistic declarative definitions to sophisticated operational automation.

Concurrently, the Helm ecosystem has witnessed the proliferation of official and community-driven chart hubs, catalyzing chart discoverability, trust, and governance. The Helm Hub, historically provided as a unified index of curated stable and incubator charts, has evolved into distributed and decentralized registries compliant with OCI (Open Container Initiative) standards. This transition enables Helm to leverage OCI artifact storage, allowing charts to be stored, versioned, and distributed like container images, increasing security by ensuring cryptographic signing and provenance tracking.

Notably, major cloud providers and open-source foundations have launched officially endorsed Helm chart repositories that align with best practices and security policies, such as the Bitnami Charts repository, Artifact Hub, and specialized registries focused on enterprise-ready charts. Artifact Hub, in particular, has become the de facto catalog aggregator, presenting thousands of Helm charts alongside other Kubernetes packaging formats like OLM bundles and Kustomize overlays. It provides filtering, rating, and automated vulnerability scanning metadata, enabling users to identify well-maintained charts with active community support.

Community-driven charts have expanded the universe of Helm usage scenarios beyond cloud-native microservices, including data science workloads, edge computing, and IoT platform deployments. These charts often serve niche technologies or customized Kubernetes distributions, underscoring Helm's extensibility. To foster quality, the community adopts stringent linting tools and continuous validation pipelines embedded in repository contribution workflows, ensuring chart correctness against evolving specification constraints.

Helm's future trajectory hints at tighter integration with cloud-native policy frameworks such as Open Policy Agent (OPA) and Kubernetes Gatekeeper, enabling policy-driven chart validation and enforcement both at installation time and runtime. Such capabilities will further elevate Helm from a pure package manager into a policy-aware delivery platform, reinforcing operational security and compliance.

The ongoing enhancements in Helm chart standards and the flourishing chart hub ecosystem collectively deliver improved reliability, security, and extensibility. These developments empower cloud-native practitioners to adopt Helm as a foundational tool in complex, multi-tenant Kubernetes environments, reliably managing application lifecycle at scale while embracing innovation in packaging and distribution practices.

10.2. Emergent Patterns: Progressive Delivery, Canary, and A/B Testing

Emerging deployment strategies leverage intelligent automation and finely grained control to reduce risks associated with software releases while optimizing feature validation and user experience. Progressive delivery, automated canary analysis, and real-time A/B testing represent a triad of complementary approaches that enhance observability, allow dynamic risk mitigation, and enable data-driven decision-making in modern continuous delivery pipelines. Their implementation often integrates declarative infrastructure as code practices, where Helm and its extensible chart format provide an effective mechanism for parametrizing and orchestrating these strategies within Kubernetes environments.

Progressive delivery delineates deployment into controlled phases, incrementally exposing new software versions to subsets of users or infrastructure endpoints. This cautious exposure contrasts with traditional all-at-once releases, reducing blast radius in case of defects. In Kubernetes ecosystems, progressive delivery depends heavily on advanced traffic management and observability signals.

Helm charts facilitate this process by enabling the templating of deployment manifests that define multiple phases: initial candidate rollout, metric-based evaluation, and automated promotion or rollback. By extending Helm values with parameters governing exposure percentages, target namespaces, and custom probes, operators gain the ability to declaratively shape rollout strategies. For example, a typical Helm values snippet for progressive delivery might look like:

```
progressiveDelivery:
  enabled: true
  rolloutPhases:
    - name: canary
      duration: 10m
      trafficPercentage: 10
      analysisTemplates:
        - successRateCheck
    - name: rollout
      duration: 20m
      trafficPercentage: 100
      analysisTemplates:
        - latencyCheck
```

Coupling these parameters with supporting chart templates that configure Kubernetes objects (Deployments, Services, Ingress, or ServiceMesh configurations) creates a tightly integrated rollout pipeline. Tools like Argo Rollouts or Flagger can be referenced within Helm charts, facilitating progressive control loops responsive to runtime metrics.

Canary deployments represent a core element of progressive delivery: a candidate version coexists with the stable release, receives a fraction of traffic, and is monitored for regressions. The challenge lies in robust, automated analysis of performance, error rates, and user experience metrics to decide promotion or rollback.

Automated canary analysis (ACA) frameworks integrate with telemetry systems such as Prometheus, Grafana, or proprietary monitoring to gather quantitative KPIs. Advanced implementations use customizable metric templates and thresholds embedded in Helm chart values, enabling consistent and version-controlled canary specifications.

A minimal example of such canary configuration within a Helm extension might be:

```
canaryAnalysis:
  metrics:
    - name: request-success-rate
      threshold: 99.5
      interval: 30s
    - name: p99-latency
      threshold: 500ms
      interval: 30s
  maxTraffic: 20
  analysisInterval: 1m
  maxAnalysisRuns: 5
```

Underneath, Helm templates generate or patch Kubernetes custom resource definitions (CRDs) such as `Rollout` resources managed by Argo Rollouts or Flagger, which perform real-time traffic shifting and integrate with metric providers to execute the ACA logic. This automation drastically reduces manual intervention and accelerates failure detection.

Real-time A/B testing constitutes an experimental deployment pattern, where two or more application variants run concurrently, with traffic routed according to configurable percentages, enabling statistical comparison of user engagement or business metrics.

A/B testing complements canary deployments in that it focuses on validating hypotheses about user experience or revenue impact rather than solely reliability.

Helm's value-driven templating is especially powerful here: it enables parameterization of variant-specific manifests and traffic split configurations, often integrating service mesh capabilities such as Istio or Linkerd for fine-grained routing control. An example partial Helm values snippet directing Istio VirtualService routing for A/B test variants might be as follows:

```
abTesting:
  enabled: true
  variants:
    - name: variant-a
      weight: 60
      imageTag: stable
    - name: variant-b
      weight: 40
      imageTag: experimental
```

Corresponding Helm templates produce Kubernetes manifests that define multiple Deployments or StatefulSets, corresponding Services, and Istio VirtualService resources enforcing traffic routing. By versioning these configurations within charts, teams achieve reproducible and auditable A/B testing setups.

Maximizing effectiveness requires integration between deployment automation, telemetry, and decision-making systems. Helm charts often include CRD manifests, hooks, and annotations that trigger external operators or continuous delivery controllers. For example, embedding annotations in Helm-managed manifests can enable controllers like Flagger to automatically initiate canary analysis and promotion workflows without additional scripting.

```
metadata:
  annotations:
    flagger.app/canary: "true"
    flagger.app/metric-provider: "prometheus"
    flagger.app/analysis-interval: "1m"
```

Automated rollbacks and promotions depend on the completeness and accuracy of underlying metrics and their thresholds, demanding thoughtful experiment design and continuous feedback loops. Progressive delivery pipelines frequently incorporate feature flags, observability dashboards, and alerting, all declaratively embedded in Helm values and templates to assure consistency and version control.

Unified management of progressive delivery, canary analysis, and A/B testing via Helm chart extensions delivers several distinct benefits:

- **Reproducibility and auditability**: Declarative artifacts version-controlled in Helm charts ensure deployment patterns and traffic shift criteria are consistent and traceable.

- **Automation-friendly**: Integration points via annotations and CRDs enable seamless interplay with operators and controllers, reducing manual effort.

- **Extensibility**: Helm's templating and values mechanisms allow pattern customization for diverse applications, metric providers, and service meshes.

- **Risk mitigation**: Fine-grained, phased exposure coupled with automated monitoring minimizes failure impacts.

- **Data-driven validation**: Real-time A/B testing embedded in deployment pipelines empowers informed decisions about feature efficacy without sacrificing reliability.

These emergent deployment patterns represent a critical evolution in continuous delivery for cloud-native architectures, effectively balancing velocity with safety through a unified, declarative infrastructure approach. Helm and chart extensions constitute a natural foundation for integrating progressive delivery, canary analysis, and A/B testing into enterprise-grade CI/CD tooling.

10.3. Integrating Service Meshes and Network Policies

The convergence of service mesh architectures and advanced Kubernetes networking paradigms introduces a nuanced landscape for orchestrating secure, resilient, and scalable microservice environments. In this context, Helm-driven deployments serve as critical enablers for managing the complexity inherent in service mesh configurations alongside finely grained network policy enforcement. This section delves into the intricate challenges and emerging opportunities when integrating Helm with service meshes such as Istio, Linkerd, or Consul, particularly under zero-trust security frameworks and sophisticated policy management regimes.

Service meshes inherently add a control plane abstraction that governs service-to-service communication by injecting sidecar proxies into application pods. These sidecars intercept network traffic, providing functionalities such as mutual TLS (mTLS), traffic routing, observability, and policy enforcement. Helm charts streamline the installation and lifecycle management of these complex components, encapsulating multi-manifest deployments and parameterized configurations. However, this abstraction and orchestration layering presents both operational difficulties and strategic possibilities.

One primary challenge lies in the synchronization of Helm values with the evolving configuration needs of the service mesh control plane and data plane proxies. In scenarios involving zero-trust networking models, every service communication requires stringent verification and authentication, enforced via policies embedded in the mesh. Helm values must therefore dynamically incorporate identity, trust anchors, and network policies that define permissible communication paths. This dynamic engagement mandates an iterative deployment workflow wherein Helm releases are tightly coupled with service mesh control plane APIs to avoid drift or misconfiguration. Helm's template-driven model must accommodate the propagation of environment-specific certificates, service identities, and selector labels for policy application without introducing manual steps that risk inconsistencies.

Furthermore, network policies designed with Kubernetes NetworkPolicy objects often require augmentation or re-implementation through mesh-specific policy constructs. While Kubernetes NetworkPolicies regulate pod-level ingress and egress traffic, service meshes provide additional enforcement capabilities tied to application layer semantics, such as HTTP route-level access control and request-level authorization. Helm-driven deployments must thus carefully manage coexistence and precedence between native Kubernetes policies and service mesh policies to prevent contradictory rules or unintended traffic exposures. Automated Helm hooks and conditional manifests can be used to deploy layered policies sequentially, enabling a predictable order of enforcement within complex service topologies.

From an operational standpoint, Helm charts for service meshes must incorporate mechanisms for policy versioning and rollback. The rapid pace of policy evolution in response to emerging threat models or shifting compliance requirements necessitates the ability to rollback or patch mesh configurations seamlessly. Helm's release management facilitates this by encapsulating policy changes as part of versioned releases, often integrated in CI/CD pipelines that automate both mesh sidecar and policy artifact updates. However, the partial update of mesh components-e.g., updating policies without restarting proxies-remains a sensitive task that requires Helm charts to leverage mesh APIs supporting live reconfiguration.

Opportunities emerge when Helm-driven deployments are combined with declarative, GitOps-style workflows. In such environments, the entire stack of service mesh configurations, network policies, and related Helm values can be described as version-controlled manifests. This approach promotes traceability, repeatability, and auditability essential for zero-trust governance. Additionally, Helm's templating and parameterization empower operators to model multi-tenant or multi-environment scenarios, embedding custom policy templates that adjust behavior automatically based on context. This scalability is crucial for enterprises managing thousands of microservices with differentiated trust domains and compliance boundaries.

A conceptual example of Helm integration within a zero-trust service mesh deployment might contain a templated Helm values file controlling mTLS enforcement, policy bindings, and selector labels:

```
global:
  meshConfig:
    enableAutoMtls: true
  policy:
    peerAuthentication:
      mtlsMode: STRICT
    authorizationPolicy:
      - name: "allow-internal-services"
        namespace: "default"
        selector:
          matchLabels:
            app: "internal-service"
        rules:
          - to:
              - operation:
                  methods: ["GET", "POST"]
                  paths: ["/api/*"]
```

This configuration snippet illustrates how Helm templating can parameterize critical aspects of mesh authentication and authorization policies, allowing fine-grained control on a per-deployment basis. Automation scripts leveraging Helm's upgrade capabilities can programmatically apply tailored policies suited for each environment-from development sandboxes to hardened production clusters.

The integration of Helm-driven deployments with service meshes underpinned by zero-trust networking principles and advanced policy management creates a rich operational domain. While the challenges center on synchronization, policy conflict resolution, and staged updates, the capabilities of Helm's templating, versioning, and automation unlock powerful operational benefits. These include scalable policy governance, environment-specific configuration management, and robust compliance adherence, positioning Helm as a fundamental tool in the secure, observable, and reliable delivery of cloud-native applications at scale.

10.4. Helm and Cross-Platform Kubernetes Management

Helm serves as the de facto package manager for Kubernetes, streamlining application deployment and lifecycle management through the use of Helm charts-preconfigured templates defining Kubernetes resource manifests. Its role expands significantly when addressing the challenges posed by hybrid, multi-cloud, and edge Kubernetes environments, where application orchestration must contend with heterogeneous infrastructure, diverse networking conditions, and inconsistent operational models.

Central to Helm's utility in cross-platform management is its abstraction layer, which decouples application definitions from the underlying Kubernetes clusters. This abstraction enables operators to define, version, and distribute application configurations that can be deployed uniformly across multiple, geographically dispersed clusters. Helm's templating engine allows for parameterization and conditional resource rendering, providing the flexibility necessary to adapt to cluster-specific requirements such as differing storage classes, ingress controllers, or resource quotas.

In hybrid cloud scenarios, where workloads are partitioned between on-premises data centers and public cloud providers, Helm facilitates consistent application deployment by encapsulating cluster-specific overrides within values files. Operators can maintain a single Helm chart repository and tailor deployments through configuration layers without duplicating chart definitions. This not only mitigates configuration drift but also accelerates rollout and rollback operations across environments with divergent policies and compliance mandates.

Multi-cloud Kubernetes deployments benefit from Helm's integration with Continuous Integration and Continuous Deployment (CI/CD) pipelines, supporting federated workflows through GitOps practices. By combining Helm with tools like Flux or Argo CD, organizations achieve declarative, version-controlled application delivery over multiple clusters and cloud providers. Helm charts stored in dedicated chart repositories become the single source of truth, enhancing auditability and reproducibility. These workflows enable automatic synchronization and remediation, which are paramount for managing at scale where manual operations are impractical.

Edge computing introduces further complexity due to limited connectivity, constrained resources, and intermittent availability. Helm's design allows for package bundling and offline installation, which is critical for edge nodes that may experience network partitioning. Operators can prepackage Helm charts, including all dependencies, and utilize secure, air-gapped mechanisms to distribute applications. The parameterized nature of Helm charts supports tailoring configurations for low-latency, resource-scarce environments typical of edge deployments, such as adjusting replica counts or resource requests dynamically.

Federation in Kubernetes, aimed at providing unified management across multiple clusters, complements Helm's capabilities by enabling consistent policy enforcement and workload distribution at scale. Projects such as Kubernetes Federation v2 (KubeFed) extend the Kubernetes API to accommodate resource propagation and lifecycle synchronization across clusters, and Helm charts integrate as the delivery mechanism for these resources. Helm's modularity allows seamless packaging of federated resource definitions, with template logic encoding constraints and affinity rules appropriate to each cluster's characteristics.

Remote management workflows increasingly leverage Helm together with cluster management platforms like Rancher, OpenShift, or Canonical's MicroK8s, which provide centralized dashboards capable of orchestrating Helm chart deployments across heterogeneous environments. These platforms expose APIs and CLI tools that programmatically trigger Helm releases, monitor deployment status, and orchestrate automated updates. Such integration reduces the operational overhead imposed by managing disparate Kubernetes endpoints.

Moreover, Helm's rollback feature ensures resilience in cross-cluster deployments by enabling rapid reversion to previous application states if synchronization or configuration errors occur. This capability is essential in complex federated setups where inconsistent states can propagate detrimental effects rapidly across multiple environments. The revision history maintained by Helm charts encapsulates each deployment iteration, thereby facilitating troubleshooting and incremental upgrades in environments marked by high deployment velocity.

Security considerations play a pivotal role when employing Helm across multi-cluster environments. Helm v3 introduces improvements by eliminating the need for Tiller, thereby reducing attack surface and enabling integration with existing Kubernetes Role-Based Access Control (RBAC) configurations. Helm charts support embedding or referencing external secrets management systems, such as HashiCorp Vault or Sealed Secrets, to manage sensitive data securely during deployment. This approach is indispensable when managing workloads across cloud providers with divergent security postures and regulatory requirements.

Helm's templating and packaging capabilities combined with version control integration, offline deployment support, and sophisticated rollout mechanisms render it a critical enabler of cross-platform Kubernetes management. It facilitates a coherent, scalable, and secure application delivery framework that abstracts underlying infrastructure complexity, allowing organizations to harness the full potential of hybrid, multi-cloud, and edge Kubernetes deployments while embracing federation and remote operational workflows.

10.5. Research: Declarative Security and Automated Drift Remediation

Emerging research in cloud-native security and infrastructure management increasingly emphasizes the automation of policy enforcement and the minimization of manual intervention to maintain compliance. Central to these efforts is the concept of *declarative security*, which formalizes security requirements and operational constraints as a set of high-level, human-readable policies that describe the desired system state rather than prescribing procedural steps. This paradigm shift enables continuous assurance of compliance through automated reconciliation, aligning system configurations perpetually with organizational security objectives.

Declarative security policies leverage domain-specific languages (DSLs) or policy frameworks that abstract the complexity of underlying platforms, such as Kubernetes, cloud provider environments, and container orchestration systems. For instance, frameworks like Open Policy Agent (OPA) allow security articulations to be written declaratively, enabling fine-grained access control, configuration validation, and anomaly detection through policy evaluation engines. These policies serve as the single source of truth against which live infrastructure states are assessed, bridging the divide between security governance and operational execution.

A crucial research dimension focuses on *automated drift detection*, addressing the issue of configuration drift-that is, divergence between the declared security posture and the actual state of deployed resources. Such drift arises from manual changes, bugs in deployment pipelines, or dynamic system behaviors. Traditional detection mechanisms rely on periodic scans and manual audits, which are prone to latency and human error. Novel approaches integrate continuous monitoring agents and event-driven triggers that compare real-time system telemetry with declared configurations. When discrepancies are detected, they produce alerts or initiate remediation workflows, reducing the window of vulnerability.

State-of-the-art methodologies employ differential analysis techniques to improve drift detection precision. By constructing canonical models of declared policy states and continuously ingesting live configuration snapshots, these systems identify both overt and subtle deviations. Advanced implementations use graph-based representations of system components and their relationships, enabling detection of complex multi-resource policy violations that might not be apparent from isolated observations.

Automated drift remediation, or self-healing, builds upon precise drift detection by enabling the system to autonomously restore desired states without human intervention. This capability is particularly relevant for ephemeral cloud environments, where frequent updates and scaling operations can introduce transient inconsistencies. Automated remediation enforces idempotence by reapplying declarative policies or invoking corrective actions that realign configurations to their secure baselines. Remediation policies must balance assertiveness and safety to prevent cascade failures or unintended disruptions.

Research in this area explores adaptive feedback loops combining declarative policy engines with orchestration controllers to facilitate closed-loop assurance. For example, GitOps principles extend to security domains by treating declarative security manifests as version-controlled artifacts; reconciliation controllers then continuously synchronize live environments with these manifests, rolling back unauthorized changes automatically. This model harmonizes rigor in compliance with operational agility.

Moreover, the advancement of *self-healing charts*-parameterized templates describing secure application deployments alongside their remediation logic-further streamlines drift management. Helm charts and similar templating systems have been extended to embed policy constraints and remediation hooks, allowing for integrated detection and correction routines triggered by configuration changes or policy violations. This encapsulation of security logic within deployment artifacts reduces complexity and improves reproducibility.

Challenges remain in standardizing declarative security semantics across heterogeneous ecosystems and ensuring that automated remediation respects business context and risk tolerance. Research is directed towards developing formal verification methods to guarantee that remediation actions preserve system invariants and comply with organizational policies. Machine learning techniques have also been explored to predict potential drift scenarios and optimize remediation strategies by analyzing historical telemetry and incident data.

Integration with broader security information and event management (SIEM) systems and orchestration platforms amplifies the contextual awareness of drift and remediation efforts. Real-time telemetry correlation enriches drift detection with threat intelligence and anomaly analytics, enabling proactive defense mechanisms. Furthermore, open research is underway to define interoperable APIs and schemas to facilitate interaction between declarative policy engines, drift detectors, and remediation controllers, fostering ecosystem-wide collaboration and toolchain composability.

In summary, the horizon of research on declarative security and automated drift remediation converges on creating resilient, self-regulating environments where compliance is embedded into the fabric of system operations. By abstracting security goals declaratively, continuously detecting deviations precisely, and enabling automated, safe remediation, these innovations aim to drastically reduce human toil and elevate the security posture of complex cloud-native infrastructures.

10.6. Community Outlook and Helm's Place in the Cloud Native Landscape

Helm's trajectory within the cloud native ecosystem has been shaped by the continuous evolution of its governance model and community dynamics. As a project initially incubated within the Kubernetes ecosystem, Helm quickly transcended its origins to become the de facto package manager for Kubernetes workloads. Central to Helm's sustained relevance is a governance structure that embraces open collaboration, transparency, and meritocracy-principles that have fostered an active and diverse community contributing to its ongoing innovation and stability.

The Helm Steering Committee, composed of elected members representing various stakeholders including end users, vendors, and independent contributors, ensures a balanced and representative decision-making process. This committee oversees major strategic directions, release schedules, and the integration of new features or architectural revisions. The committee's role in mediating between enterprise requirements and community-driven development has been pivotal in positioning Helm as both a robust production tool and a community-first project. Importantly, the governance emphasizes inclusivity by supporting community Working Groups, which focus on specific technical or outreach areas such as security, documentation, and ecosystem integration.

Over time, the Helm contributor base has matured alongside

the product's technical scope. Early contributions centered around core functionality-chart templating, dependency management, and release lifecycle operations-whereas current community efforts extend deeply into areas like enhanced security posture (e.g., support for OCI registries), multi-cluster management capabilities, and smoother workflows for Continuous Integration/Continuous Deployment (CI/CD) integrations. The Helm Hub's convergence into the Artifact Hub further exemplifies the community's adaptability, promoting a unified marketplace for Kubernetes-ready applications and fostering collaboration across tooling projects.

Helm's strategic fit in the increasingly complex cloud native landscape must be viewed relative to contemporaneous tooling advancements, particularly those addressing Kubernetes configuration management and deployment automation challenges. While alternative solutions such as Kustomize, Operators, and GitOps frameworks (e.g., Flux, Argo CD) have emerged with distinct approaches, Helm's chart-centric paradigm remains uniquely powerful for packaging and distributing pre-configured applications. Helm's templating language and strong hooks system facilitate not only straightforward application bundling but also sophisticated lifecycle management hooks and conditional logic, which are less intuitive or absent in some competing solutions.

The relationship between Helm and GitOps deserves special attention. GitOps practices emphasize declarative management of infrastructure and applications through Git repositories as single sources of truth. Helm complements GitOps workflows by enabling complex application templates to be rendered and deployed systematically from version-controlled charts. Projects such as Helm Controller-a Kubernetes controller designed to reconcile Helm charts from Git repositories-bridge the gap between Helm's packaging abilities and GitOps' operational philosophy, enabling more automated, observable, and scalable deployment pipelines.

Additionally, next-generation Kubernetes tooling is embracing extensibility and composability, often through layered abstractions. Helm fits naturally within this ecosystem as an application delivery component that can be integrated with Infrastructure as Code (IaC) frameworks and policy engines. The flexibility of Helm charts to capture application dependencies, configurable parameters, and environment-specific customizations aligns strongly with the modular demands of multi-cloud and hybrid cloud environments. Moreover, Helm's community-driven enhancement proposals (CHIPs) regularly address emerging integration points, platform security evolution, and performance improvements to maintain alignment with Kubernetes' rapid development cycles.

For organizations contemplating long-term adoption of Helm, several guiding considerations emerge. Foremost, the maturity and broad adoption of Helm provide a compelling argument for its inclusion in any cloud native operational toolkit. The rich ecosystem of curated charts reduces duplicative effort and accelerates deployment cycles, while the extensible design enables tailoring to specific performance, security, and compliance needs. It is critical, however, to remain aware of the evolving landscape-including the rise of declarative, policy-driven deployment mechanisms-and to position Helm not as an isolated tool but as a complementary component within a holistic delivery pipeline.

Decision-makers should also factor in Helm's active and transparent development model, which ensures responsiveness to community needs and industry trends. Engagement with the Helm community, whether through contribution or participation in governance discussions, can yield insight into roadmap directions and facilitate influence on feature prioritization. This proactive involvement helps mitigate risks associated with project stagnation or fragmentation, which some other Kubernetes-related projects have faced.

Helm's sustained prominence is underpinned by its sound gov-

ernance, vibrant community evolution, and a strategic posture
that embraces integration with next-generation Kubernetes tooling and workflows. Its place within the cloud native landscape
is secured as a foundational mechanism for application packaging
and deployment, adaptable to emerging practices such as GitOps
and multi-cluster management. The project's community-driven
adaptability combined with a robust technical foundation offers
a resilient and future-proof choice for organizations seeking scalable, maintainable, and extensible Kubernetes deployment solutions.

www.ingramcontent.com/pod-product-compliance
Lightning Source LLC
Chambersburg PA
CBHW061242220326
41599CB00028B/5504